Closeness To Hashem [GOD]

Kabbalist Rabbi

YAAKOV ADAS

There is no known book without mistakes. Therefore, I ask in every language of application if anyone has any questions, comments, clarifications, corrections, please send to: **book@simchatchaim.com**

All material used in this section may not be used for commercial purposes, but only for study and teaching.

To get this book or books and information Email me at:

book@simchatchaim.com

Copyright©All Rights Reserved to

www.simchatchaim.com

YB"S©All rights reserved to the Editor

First Edition 2023

Closeness to Hashem

Table of Contents

| Page | Chapter | Contents |

5   RABBI YAAKOV ADAS

7   **Chapter One** - The Strong Desire within Every Jew to Serve Hashem (G-D).

12   **Chapter Two** - "Hashem, Torah and the Jewish Nation are all One." The Make Up of the Jewish Soul.

18   **Chapter Three** - How Hashem Constantly Perpetuates the Whole world and Integrating this Knowledge into One's Service of Hashem.

23   **Chapter Four** - The Achievements of Torah Study and Mitzvot in the Upper Worlds, the Benefits for the Jewish Nation and How a Person Must Awaken himself to Serve Hashem, Thereby Helping the Jewish People.

30   **Chapter Five** - The Giving of Torah at Mt. Sinai. The Results of Every Hour a Jew Learns the Holy Torah, and Feelings of Closeness to

Closeness to Hashem

Hashem Resulting from Torah Study [Including Some Aspects of Belief in Hashem].

47 **Chapter Six** - The Entire Existence of the World is from the Power of Torah.

52 **Chapter Seven** - Reward in Gan Eden and punishment in Gehinnom.

57 **Chapter Eight** - The Not Entirely Erroneous Despair of Devoting Oneself to Torah Study, Due to the Worry of Failure Due to Lack of Talent or Stamina. They Still Can Succeed in Torah.

64 **Chapter Nine** - The Words of the Bach (Ohr Hachaim 47) on the Mitzvah of Torah Study.

71 **Chapter Ten** - Any Torah Study and Mitzvah Performance Joins the Soul with His Creator and Brings a Spiritual and Holy Bounty from Hashem. An Answer for Those Who Claim They Don't Feel This.

75 **Chapter Eleven** - Mitzvot Between Man and His Fellow

Closeness to Hashem

84 **Chapter Twelve** - The Greatness Acquired Through Torah Study.

102 **Chapter Thirteen** - Sacrifice for Torah study and Surrender of Things Which Prevents Vigilance in Torah study.

110 **Chapter Fourteen** – Prayer.

124 **Chapter Fifteen** - The Great Obligation to Be as Busy as Possible with the Holy Torah.

129 **Chapter Sixteen** - Mesillat Yesharim chapter 25.

135 **Chapter Seventeen** - The Great Benefits for the Entire Jewish Nation Resulting from every Individual's Cautiousness in Areas of Sanctity and Modesty (Tzniut).

157 **Chapter Eighteen** - The Prohibition of Haughtiness.

161 **Chapter Nineteen** - The Prohibition of Anger.

Closeness to Hashem

167   **Chapter Twenty** - The Advantages of Studying Torah and Serving Hashem with Joy and Excitement.

170   **Chapter Twenty-One** - References in Other Works Relevant to the Topics Discussed in this Book.

Closeness to Hashem

RABBI YAAKOV ADAS

He was born in the Beit Vagan neighborhood of Jerusalem to his father, Rabbi Yehuda Adas, Rosh Yeshivat Kol Yaakov, son of Rabbi Yaakov Adas, one of the heads of the Porat Yosef Yeshiva, a member of the Great Rabbinical Court and a member of the Chief Rabbinate Council, and grandson of Rabbi Avraham Chaim Adas. His mother, Rebbetzin Bila Rachel, is the daughter of Rabbi Dov Cohen, who was the Air Force's first military rabbi, and the great-granddaughter (on her father's side) of Simcha Mandelbaum.

In his youth he studied at the Kol Torah Yeshiva and the Kol Yaakov Yeshiva headed by his father. After his marriage, he lived in the Beit Vagan neighborhood. He studied with the Kabbalist Rabbi Yitzchak Kadouri for seven years.

Rabbi Adas is prominent in the customs of asceticism and celibacy. He rarely gets a haircut and changes his clothes. He wears a tallit at all hours of the day. Some have interpreted his wanderings between yeshivas as an "exile" he imposed on himself as some rabbis did in previous generations. He is currently staying at Rabbi David Batzri's Yeshivat Hashalom.

Rabbi Adas gives lessons from time to time in the Western Wall plaza, and other yeshivas and

Closeness to Hashem

synagogues his lessons deal with the Thalmud, Halacha in practice, morals, faith and Kabbalah.

He prays with stormy weeping and effort. In recent years, he has been the regular cantor in the Kabbalah according to the Rashash's intentions in the morning prayers at sunrise at the Western Wall. He also participates in the Midnight Tikkun every Thursday night in the Western Wall tunnels, with Rabbi Benyahu Shmueli Rosh Yeshivat Nahar Shalom.

Rabbi Yaakov Adas has authored dozens of books in various fields. He makes sure to print his books without punctuation. His books also include sermons on topics such as Kabbalah, Talmud, women's modesty, education, and dealing with youths who have gone astray.

In some books and pamphlets, he claims to have supernatural powers and he teaches people in his books how to achieve such powers.

In this book he teaches and shows how everyone can be close to God.

Closeness to Hashem

Chapter One

The Strong Desire within Every Jew to Serve Hashem

1.
There exists within every Jew a deep inner desire to come close to Hashem. There are those who feel this very often and there are those who feel this less, yet the inner source for this resides within every Jew.

2.
The medrash writes, "When the Holy Temple was being destroyed, the conquering gentiles wanted the first person to enter the Temple and plunder it be a Jew (seemingly to denigrate them even more). A Jew by the name of Yosef Meshisa took the task upon himself, entered the Holy Temple and brought out the menora. The gentiles then asked him to re-enter and bring out another item. However, this time he refused and said, "Is it not

Closeness to Hashem

sufficient that I angered my Creator once, that I should anger him again". The gentiles tried to convince him with substantial sums of money and high positions; and then threatened him with punishments and death, but he would not give in. In the end they gave him a terrible death with an axe. While they were killing him he was shouting, but not because of the terrible pain, rather he cried out, 'Woe is to me that I angered my Creator, woe is to me that I angered my Creator.'"

3.

We ask the question, where did this Jew find the strength to make such a turnaround in one short instant? Just one moment earlier he had agreed to enter the Holy Temple and plunder it, a terrible action in itself, and especially at such a difficult time for the Jewish nation. The temple was being destroyed, so many people killed, captured, wounded, starving and suffering; and at such a time to be so treacherous and enter the holiest place of the nation and plunder it! Still, one moment later he changed himself, reaching the lofty level of being killed for the sake of the glorification of Hashem's name. And even more, at the time of his death he didn't cry out due to the pain, but because he had angered his Creator!

4.

The answer is that within every Jew lies a holy soul which wants only to do the will of Hashem

Closeness to Hashem

with all its might. But, there are many coverings on the soul, which sometimes have their own desires, affecting the actions of a person. This is especially true if these urges are influenced by an environment which does not follow the way of Hashem. Therefore, even this Jew, who stooped so low as to enter the Holy Temple and plunder it, could in one moment affect a complete turn around. Deep within him he had a holy soul whose desire was only to serve Hashem - at any cost.

5.
The work of every Jew is to work on himself so that the sacred part within him affect his actions and behavior in order that he always go in the ways of Hashem.

6.
There are a few ways that a person can activate this. We will bring two of the main ways here. The first is that a person must know the greatness of the goodness hidden within him, and also of his great inner ability to reach high levels in serving Hashem. The second way is that a person must know the profound results of his every action, word, intention, thought or desire for good.

7.
There is no doubt that if every Jew were to recognize these two strengths within him, in their entirety, this knowledge alone would bring him enormous strength. He would withstand all tests

Closeness to Hashem

and serve his Creator with all his might, day and night. It could also be that he would manage to avoid the spiritual pitfalls of this world. However, it is usually not within our power to fully recognize our resources. Still it follows that the more a person knows about his abilities, and tries to strengthen them, his desire to serve his Creator will intensify and increase.

Closeness to Hashem
Chapter Two

"Hashem, Torah and the Jewish Nation are all One."

The Make Up of the Jewish Soul

1.
The RamChal in his book 'Adir Bamorom' and also in the 'Nefesh Hachaim' (4:11), and many other books bring the quote from the 'Zohar'; "The Holy One Blessed Be He, Torah and Yisrael are all one, since Hashem, the Torah and the Jewish nation are the same thing". [This expression has not been found in the Zohar - it seems that they intended to explain a similar expression written in the Zohar.]

2.
These words require explanation. How can it be possible to say this? Hashem has neither body nor body form; He fills and rotates all the worlds. The Torah is the holy Torah scroll and Yisrael are human beings. How is it therefore possible to say that they are all the same thing?

Closeness to Hashem

3.

A preface is essential here to explain this matter. Man is comprised of body and soul. Everyone knows and feels what the body is. Similarly, everyone knows intuitively that the soul exists within the body, since the difference between a live and a dead person is quite obvious, still it is extremely difficult to ultimately define what the soul is. We can explain the little that we know about the soul with a parable of sun rays extending from the sun, their whole existence sourced in the sun. Were a person to place a board in the middle of the sun beam, isolating it from its source, the sun, it would cease to shine beyond the board (at least those parts which cannot travel through the board, meaning all those which are visible to the eye). This is true also of a Jewish soul. The soul extends from Hashem (obviously the parable and it's moral are completely different, since the actual distance between the soul and The Creator is immeasurable and totally incomparable to the much smaller distance between the sun and it's rays. The purpose of the parable is simply to illustrate that the ray's entire existence is drawn from this source.) In truth, everything in the world receives its existence from Hashem and although this is not the place to speak lengthily about this, the soul of a Jew is more directly sourced in Hashem and can feel its connection more.

Closeness to Hashem

4.

Let us return to our topic, to explain the aforementioned saying, that Hashem, the Torah and the Jewish nation are all one thing. It means that the souls of the Jewish nation are a bounty of spiritual light. (In Kabbalistic books, spiritual bounty is always referred to with expressions of shining or light, one of the reasons being that in the physical world, the most spiritual thing is light and it is also something completely good. There are of course many other deeper reasons for the use of this expression which shortage of space does not permit us to bring here.) This goodness extends from Hashem himself, who is the Source of the light. This explains how Hashem and the Jewish nation can be one thing - one is the source and the other is the result.

5.

To understand how the Torah is one with Hashem and the Jewish nation we need to know a basic principle brought in many places in Chazal. The gemarah in Sanhedrin 99 explains on the verse; "A soul labors, the labor is for him" [to clarify the double expression of labor in the verse] 'He works in this area and the Torah works for him in another area'. Rashi explains that when a person labors over Torah, the Torah requests that Hashem help him understand Torah. Clearly Torah is not just a physical scroll that we have here in this world, but

Closeness to Hashem

the Torah exists spiritually in the higher worlds and is able to request things of Hashem (a well-known comparison to this is the spiritual existence of angels).

6.
According to this, we can now understand how the Torah is also one with Hashem and Yisrael. Hashem structured the world in a way that the bounty coming from Him to the Jewish soul, is carried via the spiritual existence of Torah, as the bounty is created within it. The formation of the souls of Yisrael is brought about and carried via the beam of the holy Torah which is also a type of extension of Hashem (as explained in the words of the Ramchal in his book, 'Adir Bamorom', described here in a general way, without full detail).

7.
There is an additional point here. There is a strong inner longing within the soul of every human being is to have a greater connection with its source, and receive more goodness and strength for the soul. The way to merit this, according to the aforementioned saying, is to increase one's commitment to Torah, including all areas of the service of Hashem detailed in the Torah. These includes keeping mitzvot, distancing oneself from sin between man and Hashem and between man and his fellow man, and also strengthening oneself

Closeness to Hashem

in prayer. This will increase one's spiritual bounty and as a result, the higher bounty will be stimulated to shine on him through the light of Torah.

8.

When a person thinks properly about these things, they will awaken a great desire in his heart to study Torah and fulfill the will of Hashem in all areas. Through this his soul becomes connected to its source and receives additional light similar to the light his soul already has. This is really what the soul longs for, more than all other desires of this world. We see this in Mesillat Yesharim (chapter 1), "The soul is way above all, its true enjoyment is only to bask in the light of Hashem's face."

Chapter Three

How Hashem Constantly Perpetuates the Whole world and Integrating this Knowledge into One's Service of Hashem

1.
"In the beginning the Lord created the heavens and the earth". There are many fundamental differences between Hashem creating the world and a person forming an item. One of these differences is that Hashem created the entire world from absolutely nothing, whereas a person can only produce an item from something that already exists, by cutting and joining things together. Another difference is that when a person produces an item, the moment that the production process is completed, the item stands independent of it's producer. In contrast, Hashem recreates the whole world at every moment, just as He did when He

Closeness to Hashem

originally created the world. If He were to choose to destroy the world, He would not need to use something to destroy it; rather it would be enough to simply cease recreating the world. The Nefesh Hachaim deals with this at length (shaar 1 and 3).

2.

He writes (shaar 1: chapter 2) that the way of Hashem is different to the ways of man. A person who builds a building from wood does not create and generate the wood from his energy, rather he simply takes the pre-existing wood and puts them in a specific building order. When everything is organized the way he wants it to be, he can forget about the building and still it will not cease to exist. However, Hashem does as he did at the creation of the world. He created and produced everything from absolutely nothing with His infinite strength and abundant light. Were Hashem to deny the world His energy and bounty for even one moment, it would instantly return to nothingness and emptiness. In shaar 3: chapter 11, the Nefesh Hachaim writes that this is one of the basic principles of belief in Hashem; every Jew must fix in his heart that Hashem is the true and only power, that He is the soul, the life provider and source of every person and creation, and all forces and worlds.

3.

In shaar 3: chapter 11, he elaborates further that

Closeness to Hashem

the whole world was formed by the command of Hashem, as recorded in parshat Bereishit. For each thing Hashem said that it would be, and so it was. The word of Hashem is a real spiritual entity with power to generate the entire existence of the world. He explains further that the spiritual reality of Hashem's word is eternal and does not end with the days of creation. These continuously existing commands sustain and support everything in the world, like the living soul of all existence.

4.

He also writes on the verse in Yeshayahu (40:5), "And all flesh together will see that the mouth of Hashem has spoken". "The verse refers to the future time when Hashem's supervision will be so clear, until we merit literally seeing with our physical eyes, how the word of Hashem is spread out over every thing sustaining it" - see the text inside for his full essay.

5.

He adds that there was already a sample glimpse of this concept at Mt. Sinai at the giving of the Torah. This is referred to in the verse in Parshat Yitro (20:18), "And all the people saw the sounds" [The simple meaning here is the sounds which occurred uniquely at the Mt. Sinai event. But there are many ways and perceptions of the Torah, as is clear from Chazal, and there are many understandings to every verse given at Sinai.

Closeness to Hashem

There are the simple meanings, and the meanings which are hinted to within the words, that which can be expounded from it, and the hidden secrets of it]. Here the sounds refer to the sounds of the word of Hashem at the time of the creation of the world, meaning that they merited seeing how this voice is the soul of the creation, sustaining it in its entirety. See how this is explained later in the chapter of the giving of the Torah at Mt. Sinai.

6.

This knowledge greatly enables a person to feel how he is constantly close to Hashem. Through thinking and contemplating about this, a person can come to see the hand of Hashem and its influences at every moment and in every area. He should not however feel that it is sufficient to study this concept just once, rather the more he repeats it to himself and regulates his thoughts towards it, so too will the results increase and he will come to feel closeness to Hashem.

Chapter Four

The Achievements of Torah Study and Mitzvot in the Upper Worlds, the Benefits for the Jewish Nation and How a Person Must Awaken himself to Serve Hashem, Thereby Helping the Jewish People

1.
It is clear from the holy Zohar and other Kabbalistic books that apart from our world, Hashem created many countless multitudes of worlds and higher spiritual energies. Through the mitzvot and good deeds of the Jewish nation, these worlds are built up and established, resulting in a great pouring of spiritual and physical goodness to the entire Jewish nation. On the other hand, by not learning Torah and through other transgressions,

Closeness to Hashem

the opposite of this is achieved.

2.

The fact that there are higher worlds is a basic principle of Torat HaKabbalah. The state of our world and the state of the upper worlds are interdependent. As mentioned earlier, the state of the upper worlds is determined by our deeds in this world. So too the condition of the upper worlds determines the state of this world.

3.

In the Nefesh Hachaim (shaar 1: chapter 4) we see that the destruction of the Holy Temple followed this pattern too. Through the bad deeds of the Jewish nation, the Holy Temple of the higher spiritual worlds was destroyed, and since the higher Holy Temple was destroyed due to our transgressions, the gentiles were able to wield their power over the Holy Temple on temple mount and destroy it.

4.

The same is true of the exile of the nation from their homeland, with the land of Israel left in the hands of gentiles. It was the sinning of Yisrael which blemished the upper spheres corresponding to the holiness of the land of Israel. The land was then easily delivered into the hands of the gentiles.

5.

The Nefesh Hachaim continues (shaar 1: chapter 4) and says; "This is the power of the Torah. A

Closeness to Hashem

Jewish person should never say, 'What am I? What strength do I have to achieve anything with my lowly actions?' Rather he should know, understand and implant in his mind and heart, that every detail of his actions, words and thoughts at every moment are never destroyed. As much as he multiplies his actions and increases and elevates them, so too each one will rise towards it's roots, fulfilling it's purpose in the upper higher realms, honing the lofty lights." We see that a person must give thought to fully preserving his strengths for learning Torah and keeping mitzvot, since every mitzvah that he does achieves incredible things for the good of all the worlds.

6.

On the other hand, "… in truth, when a wise person pays attention to his deeds which are not so good, and he understands this reality, his heart will quiver inside him with a great trembling, when he sees how easily a slight transgression, Hashem forbid, can corrupt and destroy."

7.

I once heard a parable for this. A person sitting in a missile control room can press a button and shoot a missile injuring and killing the enemy, thereby saving his whole country. Alternatively, he could mistakenly press an incorrect button and kill some of his own countrymen. When people come to either praise him for his heroic deeds or

Closeness to Hashem

to accuse him for his unscrupulous actions, he reasons, "What have I done? I simply pressed a button!" His mistake is that he doesn't realize that it is no ordinary button; rather it is fully installed and programmed in a way that through a tiny action one can produce terrible results.

8.

Accordingly, when a person is busy with Torah he helps the entire Jewish nation; he secures the upper worlds causing an increase in the outpouring of blessing and success for all of Yisrael. Sometimes a person learns for an hour and when he finishes, he feels that he didn't really do enough in this hour. The truth is who knows what salvation he succeeded in bringing to the Jews with this hour of learning? It is even possible that he saved many Jews from death, or perhaps many ill people were healed in his merit. This is not necessarily just from studying of Torah, it is the same with every mitzvah that a person does. However, the power of Torah study is especially great, as Chazal say in the mishna in massechet Peah, "… and the study of Torah is equal to all of them." Apart from learning Torah and performing mitzvot, there is also abstaining from transgressions. A person thus helps the entire Jewish nation. [See the Nefesh Hachaim, shaar four from chapter eleven until the end of the shaar where he explains extensively about this topic as

Closeness to Hashem

he does in the earlier chapters of the book.]

9.

It says in massechet Yevamot that compassion and loving kindness are special attributes of the Jewish nation. Within every Jew lie feelings of great compassion for those who are suffering, and also a great desire to help them. Therefore, when a person stands uncertain whether to use the next hour for the study of Torah or to waste it doing something else, even if he does not merit to have the conviction to decide to learn because of the obligation to learn Torah, he can still try to decide in favor Torah study due to his desire to help his suffering brethren. His learning can aid them. Even though he cannot know who he has helped and which type of deliverance he brought about, still the words of Chazal are absolutely true. He has definitely benefited the Jewish nation.

Chapter Five

The Giving of Torah at Mt. Sinai.

The Results of Every Hour a Jew Learns the Holy Torah, and Feelings of Closeness to Hashem Resulting from Torah Study [Including Some Aspects of Belief in Hashem]

1.
The giving of the Torah at Mt. Sinai is described at length in the Torah in parshat Yitro - see the text inside for full detail. It is impossible to elaborate here about this; however, we will, with Hashem's help, explain one point of the Mt. Sinai event focused upon in many of our holy books. We will also bring what there is to learn from it regarding the study of Torah, and in general in the service of Hashem

Closeness to Hashem

2.

The purpose of this book is not to bring proofs about belief in Hashem, rather to explicate ways of coming close to serving Hashem. Still the topic of this chapter is about the Mt. Sinai event, so we will elucidate here a little of what there is to say on this happening, together with some points of belief in Hashem. There is a fundamental difference between the Jewish religion and other religions. They are based on revelations experienced by one man or a group of individuals. This being the case, each religion is dependant upon the agreement to believe those people that they are not lying. Whoever is familiar with the details of the stories of these religions, knows that ordinary logic cannot accept their report. It is difficult to elaborate here and bring their mistakes and show the awesome incongruity within them. We can however bring how the Jewish religion and the incredible revelation at Sinai are reported clearly in the Torah. It happened in front of millions of people! It is written that it was before about six hundred thousand males over the age of twenty, which together with their wives is approximately one million two hundred thousand people, and together with those under the age of twenty this comes to more than two million, plus the mixed multitude who joined the Jews when they left Egypt. One simply cannot fabricate such

Closeness to Hashem

a story. If one were to come and say that he had witnessed a creature which has never been seen or heard of before, whoever wants to believe him can and whoever doesn't want to believe him doesn't. On the other hand was this individual to claim that he saw this creature together with millions of other people who also saw it, the listener will then ask where these millions of people are hiding! If it is true and millions say that they did see this creature then it proves that they all saw correctly, since why would millions of people lie? And especially about something as obligating as the yoke of Torah and mitzvot.

3.

This is the reason why the biggest religions all based themselves on the Mt. Sinai event and on Judaism. They just changed later events to produce a new religion, using intelligence insulting lies. It is surprising why they chose to use the Jewish religion to build upon. It is something which creates the most questions about their religions, since if they agree that at the beginning Judaism was the true religion, how can a change be justified with their illogical reasoning? [This also explains the great hatred that they have for the Jewish nation. The very existence of a Jewish nation invalidates their religion. The intellect cannot accept such a huge adjustment.] They built upon Judaism

Closeness to Hashem

rationalizing that at least the first stage of their religion should be based on something that logic obligates one to accept. The Torah of Israel, where the Sinai revelation was in front of millions of people, is irrefutable and therefore the only way to start off with something absolutely true.

4.

One cannot therefore question why there are so many amongst the scholars of the wisdom of the world who don't hold of Torah. It's not really a problem since we see with our own eyes that there are learned people who nowadays try to disprove the holocaust, even though the denials stand against all logic. Whenever someone has a personal agenda about something he can speak completely irrational things, all in the name of science. His agenda causes him speak differently to what he really knows to be true. Sometimes his personal desires will even change the way he thinks. A person can have many different types of agenda. In our case it could be that it is hard for him to change his behavior. There are many other reasons too; lack of place does not permit elaboration here. We can however note the verse, "Bribery blinds the eyes of the wise and makes crooked the words of the righteous." The following questions are brought in the name of the Goan; 1) What is the double expression here - 'it blinds the eyes of the wise' and 'makes crooked

Closeness to Hashem

the words of the righteous'?, 2) How can we understand the change in expression here? The first speaks about 'blinding eyes' and the second about 'making words crooked' and 3) Why is it that the first time the verse refers to 'the wise' and the second to 'righteous'? He explains that when there is a judgment, the success of the judges to decide the matter properly is dependant on two things. The first is to thoroughly understand the reality of what happened. The second is to clarify the halachic ruling in such a situation. The verse says that bribes change both of these things; how one perceives the entire reality of an occurrence. This explains the use of the expression, 'blinding of eyes', and also the expression of 'wise' since it is not relevant what his level in Torah is. Bribery also changes one's understanding of the halachic rulings for the pertinent situation. This explains the use of the expression, 'making crooked'; it refers to the words and tongues of righteous people whose knowledge of Torah is their righteousness. This is so true in our case. A private agenda can transform logic, even having actually seen an event. When it comes to understanding the final outcome, one must take from the strength of the reality.

5.

In general, it is worthwhile to know that in every field of worldly wisdom there are two types of

Closeness to Hashem

wisdom; theoretic science, which includes all the philosophical topics etc., and practical science which includes physical topics e.g. physics etc. In one university it is possible to find many different professors teaching practical sciences. One professor teaches according to one belief, and one professor teaches according to another. One teaches atheism in one way and another teaches it in another way. When one thinks carefully about this, it turns out that even without knowing as we do that only Judaism is true, that all their words are meaningless. We see it from their very own words! It must be that no more than one of them can be correct and all the others are completely mistaken. If so, how can it be that all of them are professors? It must be that a high position in theoretical sciences is not dependant on the degree of correctness of a person's words, rather on the way that he can present his opinion. Rather he is judged whether he gives over the subject in an interesting way and in a way that the students will be able to repeat over his words. [There are topics in science that are compiled partly of theoretical science and partly of practical science, meaning that the first part of the proof to their opinion is based on experiments and part is based on their own reasoning. Much of what they say about nature is of this type. Therefore, regarding faith, their words have no more strength than theoretical

Closeness to Hashem

science. No factory owner will agree to invest money in an expensive but risky production, since it is not normal to invest in something that is doubtful, only something certain. A person would only agree to invest if he was presented with proofs which are from start to finish based on experiments.

6.
There is much more to prove and clarify in various aspects of belief, for which there is no place here to elaborate. Perhaps with the help of Hashem I will be able to write about this in greater length in another place. Here we have deviated to this only in order to illustrate some of what there is to learn from the Mt. Sinai event to help in the service of Hashem.

Closeness to Hashem

For the Service of Hashem

Part two

1.
Let us return to our topic, what there is to take from knowing of the details of the occurrences at Mt. Sinai (apart from all the revelations enumerated in the verses in parshat Yitro) to aid one's service of Hashem and learning Torah. The Holy One Blessed Be He showed the Jews something amazing. They actually felt how everything that in the world is all rooted in Hashem and a continuation of Him. There is nothing apart from Hashem that has its own existence. In fact, at every moment everything in the world is maintained by the Creator and nourished from Him. This point is brought also in the Nefesh Hachaim in shaar 3: chapter 11. [Some of which is brought here in chapter 3.] See what is written there in the Nefesh Hachaim, hinting to this from the words of the verse - this is not the place to elaborate on it.

2.
We can explain with a parable. Reuven came and claimed to Shimon that their friend Levi is not a

Closeness to Hashem

person at all, rather he is a robot activated by spies from another country. Shimon will bring hundreds of proofs why this just doesn't make sense etc. etc. However, were Reuven to come and speak to Shimon himself about Shimon, that Reuven has found out about him that he is not a person, rather a robot, Shimon need not bring any proofs that this is not true, since Shimon knows who and what he is. He knows that he is a person with a soul etc. etc. So too with the Mt. Sinai event. Every person felt completely, with his own feelings, knowledge and perception, how his entire existence and being is something coming from Hashem, in a most undeniable way.

3.
In truth even without being at Mt. Sinai, if a person were to merit really knowing his own soul, he would automatically know with an absolute knowledge that he is created by the Creator of the world, and drawn entirely from Him. He would see clearly that the whole entity of his soul is something nurtured from the Creator Himself and is a continuation from Him. [This refers to everything, not just the soul, but with the soul it is more direct.]

4.
There are many people who have this feeling, or at any rate something of it in a small measure. Fortunate is the one who merits to this. This

Closeness to Hashem

feeling can bring a person to have a great attachment to Hashem. It is still true that someone who does not merit this feeling can still attain incredible levels of being attached to Hashem. [In truth, even those who claim to have not experienced this feeling, most of them have in some measure had it. It just was not the strength that they wanted, so they missed out on the feeling.] In short, not everyone feels this reality in a strong and definite way, and this is part of the concealment of the soul by the body in this world.

5.

One who has not previously merited to this feeling can merit it via various methods. One of these ways is thorough the study of the holy Torah. There are many reasons why studying Torah brings this. One is [the following is partly based on the book of R' Shmuel Rossovsky Zatzal, on massechet Makot at the end of the new edition] that the intensity of this feeling in its fullness was experienced by the whole Jewish nation at Mt. Sinai. The Nefesh Hachaim writes in shaar 4: chapter 14 on the topic of learning Torah (slightly adapted) that every moment one is busy with and bonded to Torah as he should, the words rejoice as they did when they were given at Sinai. It says in the Zohar at the beginning of parshat Chukat [in the Targum] that whoever puts effort into Torah it is as if he stands every day at Mt. Sinai, ready to

Closeness to Hashem

accept the Torah. [Note that the expression is 'whoever puts effort into Torah' - perhaps it is hinting that even if the learning was not as successful as he wanted, he still was busy with Torah and tried to study it]. Just as at the time of that holy event they were joined, to the word of Hashem, so to speak, so too at this moment. Every single time a person is busy with Torah and toils over it; he connects to the word of Hashem. It is all from the mouth of Hashem. The entirety of what he told Moshe at Sinai came out of His mouth. Even what a small pupil would in the future ask his teacher was said at Sinai. Now when a person is busy with the words of Torah, each word leaps from the mouth of Hashem becoming a flame of fire, so to speak. [This does not mean physical fire, rather a holy spiritual reality. So, when it writes 'the mouth of Hashem' it is obviously an illustrative expression]. It is considered as though these words are received at this very moment from Sinai, from Hashem Himself. Therefore, Chazal say many times, "And the words will bring joy like when they were given at Mt. Sinai and then the rays of blessing will spread over all the worlds from their lofty source. The earth will also be illuminated with its light and will be blessed with its glory. It will bring many good things and outpourings of bounty to the world." The essence of the words of the Nefesh

Closeness to Hashem

Hachaim is that the inspiration that there was at the time of the giving of the Torah is repeated every time that a Jew busies himself with the study of Torah. As is understood, this is to a much lesser degree than at the time of the giving of the Torah, but it is of the same type. Therefore, through studying Torah, a person can merit in some way to the aforementioned inner feeling, where the soul feels its absolute connection to the Creator of the universe.

6.

Here are some points of what has been discussed so far:

I) There is a level of closeness to Hashem that the soul can feel with an inner intuition. It can feel its true existence; how it is a spiritual offshoot from Hashem, a spark of Hashem Himself. This is the way the soul feels a real connection with the Creator of the world.

II) At the time of the giving of the Torah, the entire Jewish nation merited this level in its totality.

III) Even after the giving of the Torah, many merits to this. The intensity and duration of the feeling depends on each individual's abilities.

IV) Even someone who has never experienced this feeling [it is possible that he in actual fact has done, but in such a smaller measure than

Closeness to Hashem

he would like] there are ways to merit it. The first way is to invest maximum efforts to be involved with Torah.

V) Even without this inner feeling it is possible to believe in Hashem with complete faith and to serve Him fervently and faithfully. The way each person serves Hashem must be according to his individual task in life, assigned to him by the Creator of the world.

VI) Know that when many holy writings speak about the topic of 'simple faith', they are referring to this very feeling. One cannot ask *if* it is possible that the soul feel its existence, that it is actually drawn from Hashem. Rather one should ask *how* the soul can feel the verity of the Torah of Israel from its very existence, and how the Torah is linked with one's identity. This is not a problem, as explained in chapter 2, since the soul of every Jew is drawn from the Creator Himself via the lights of the Torah. The soul will therefore have the strength this.

Chapter Six

The Entire Existence of the World is from the Power of Torah

1.
Chazal, in the gemarah in massechet Shabbat 88a, learn from pesukim that the Holy One Blessed Be He made a condition with the works of creation, "If Yisrael accept the Torah you will have permanence, and if not, you will return to be emptiness and void." - see there for the full detail of this conversation.

2.
The Nefesh Hachaim explains this at length in shaar 4: chapter 11. The main point of what he says is that apart from the Torah scroll that we have in this world, there is a very holy spiritual existence in the higher worlds which is also called Torah. This is the root of the Torah that we have here in this world [see chapter 2 what is explained

Closeness to Hashem

about this]. From the creation of the world until the time of the giving of the Torah at Sinai, the whole existence of this world and all the worlds was because of this spiritual existence of Torah in the higher worlds. This was the way that Hashem established the order of the creation. He made it that all bounty can only reach all the worlds through the rays of the Torah.

3.
So, from the time of the giving of the Torah there was not sufficient light from the Torah existing in the higher worlds to keep the world going. It therefore became necessary that the Jewish nation learn Torah. Through the Torah study of the Jewish people here in this world, the upper lights of the Torah in the higher worlds are strengthened. Only with this reinforcement could there be enough bounty to suffice the period after the giving of the Torah. Through Torah study the world was able to continue.

4.
The Nefesh Hachaim writes, "The truth is, without a doubt, that if the world were to be, from one end to the other be for even one moment, empty from our study and meditation of the Torah; all the worlds would be destroyed and become nothing and emptiness - Hashem forbid.

5.
Hashem has merited us so far and this vacancy has

Closeness to Hashem

never happened and the worlds have not been destroyed, as there are always people busy with Torah. Still, the increase and decrease of bounty depends on the measure and the amount of our busyness with Torah. If we hold onto the Torah with all our might, as we should, we acquire eternal life and extra sanctity and blessing and great light in all the worlds, spreading out from its source hidden high above all the worlds. It also greatly corrects and builds up anything that was previously destroyed.

6.

He brings there from Chazal that Torah scholars are the pillars of the world, as the verse says, "If not for my covenant of day and night, I would not have established the statutes of heaven and earth." They comment further on the verse, "The wisdom of the woman built her home." that Hashem said, "If a person merits to study Torah and wisdom, it is as considered before me as though he created the heavens, and as if he established the whole world." They continue, "Hashem said to Yisrael, 'My children, busy yourselves with Torah day and night and I will credit you as if you support the whole world'." See the Nefesh Hachaim itself for many more sources in Chazal for incredible things about how majorly dependent the world's existence is on the Jewish nation's learning of Torah.

Closeness to Hashem

7.
Every person must take these things to heart and review them well, [review of the Nefesh Hachaim shaar 4: chapters 11-34 are recommended]. In that way a person will value every moment of Torah study, and realize how it is something so much more important and productive than any worldly business, which appear to be such great things. The Torah is therefore descried in the pasuk; "It is more precious than pearls and all your acquisitions cannot equal it."

Chapter Seven

Reward in Gan Eden and punishment in Gehinnom

1.
The mishna in Avos says, "One hour of life in the world to come is more beautiful than an entire life in this world." This can be explained as follows; if one were to join all the worldly pleasures that have ever been and ever will be experienced by man, from the time of creation of the world until the end of time, it can still not outweigh even one moment of the pleasure that the soul has in the next world.

2.
On the other hand, it is clear from our holy books that even seventy years of afflictions like those of Iyov in this world, does not outweigh the suffering the soul feels in one moment in Gehinnom.

3.
The explanation of this is that the pleasures and

Closeness to Hashem

the pains of the world to come are much more intense than those of this world. A part explanation of this is [based partly on the words of the Ramban in his work, 'Torat Ha'adam' in the sha'ar hagemul] that one needs to clarify every area of enjoyment and suffering in this world, whether it is of the body or the soul. It cannot be true that they are only of the body, since the body of a dead person experiences neither pleasures nor suffering in such ways. It certainly cannot be true that they are purely of the soul, since pleasures and pains like eating and injuries are of the body. The answer must therefore be that enjoyment and suffering are mainly of the soul but since the soul is clothed in a body, automatically it's pleasures and pains will be clothed in physical actions.

4.

In the world to come the type of enjoyments are very different. They are more direct pleasures to the soul, without the garment of the body. It goes the other way too, and the suffering is therefore a type which hurts the soul in a much more direct way. It follows therefore that whatever goes more directly is much much greater.

5.

This can be compared to a person who disobeys a human king, and the king decrees a punishment of receiving lashes from the king himself. The king gave the sinner two choices, either five lashes with

Closeness to Hashem

a stick on his bare back, or fifty lashes with the stick whilst wearing such a thick covering that he basically cannot feel the beating. Obviously he prefers the fifty lashes with the covering rather than five without it. The same is true in our discussion here.

6.
See the Ramban in 'Torat Ha'adam' in the sha'ar hagemul [see p.386, 387 for the whole discussion, this here is just a short extract] where he writes that just as in this world fire burns the body, so too in the world too come there is a spiritual reality called fire, which is the root of fire in this world, and has the ability to burn the soul [obviously the fire in Gehinnom is not the same type of fire as in this world].

7.
Apart from what we have said about the quantity of the reward in the world to come compared to the pleasures of this world, there is a further point here; the reward in Gan Eden is eternal. The Ramchal writes that reward in the next world is not like a payment that a person pays his friend in this world, in exchange for an item that he purchased, and when the price is paid, he is exempt from any further imbursement. However, in the world to come, even though a person receives reward according to his performance of mitzvot, he still continuously receives the reward

Closeness to Hashem

because it is eternal, forever and ever and unceasing. More than this, the reward grows and increases since the reward is spiritual and holy and therefore purifies the person more and more until he becomes worthy of even more reward.

8.

The essence of a high level in serving Hashem is when a person performs mitzvot, and guards himself from aveirot out of love for Hashem and awe of His greatness, and not out of fear of punishment. Of course, every person must fear punishment and know of the great reward of mitzvot; these are great tools to save oneself from the persuasions of the evil inclination. What we have mentioned above is a noteworthy in regards to this area. But a person should know that he does not gain a thing by refraining from doing a mitzvah or by going ahead with an aveirah, because any profit in this world is worth absolutely nothing, zero, compared to the smallest amount of reward in the world to come.

Chapter Eight

The Not Entirely Erroneous Despair of Devoting Oneself to Torah Study, Due to the Worry of Failure Due to Lack of Talent or Stamina. They Still Can Succeed in Torah.

1.
There are many who in the truth of the matter very much want to devote themselves to study the holy Torah. But they hold themselves back, thinking that they have no hope succeeding greatly in amassing knowledge and understanding in Torah. This brings a person to despair from investing great effort into Torah study since the dividends do not seem to be in proportion to the investment.
2.
There are also many who seemingly want to dedicate themselves to the study of Torah but are

Closeness to Hashem

afraid that they will be unable to maintain the commitment. This fear holds them back from dedicating themselves to learning, since they think that it is worthless to be committed for a short period.

3.

In truth this approach is mistaken for a number of reasons. We see the first in the gemarah Sanhedrin 99, which comments on the verse, "The soul which toils, it will toil for him". It explains that a person who toils in Torah, Torah will labor for him in another area [it seems that the explanation here is based on the double expression of 'toiling' in the verse]. Rashi explains, "The Torah goes to Hashem and beseeches that He reveal to him the reasons in the Torah" [this topic is discussed in chapter 2 above]. It is clear that the success requested by the Torah for the person concerned, is a supernatural success, since success within the limitations of nature do not require prayer. [It is logical to deduce from here that just as the Torah requests for Torah understanding on his behalf, it also requests that he have the ability to maintain his study of Torah since they are both dependant on the illumination of the Torah joining with the light of his soul]. If he despairs of learning Torah, reasoning that it seems as if he is unable to succeed, he errs. He may be able to succeed naturally in some measure, but if he labors in

Closeness to Hashem

Torah he will merit supernatural success which he even measure.

4.

There is another reason why a low self evaluation of one's abilities is mistaken. This is from the Zohar, explained at length in the writings of the Arizal and clarified in the Nefesh Hachaim - sha'ar 4. It is a very great fundament that there are different types of soul. There are souls which are more outstanding and those which are less so and there are many different ways to explain this, but there is no place here for that. Many of the types of outstanding soul will cause an incredibly strong desire to learn Torah, so one can have great success in Torah study. It is clear in the Zohar and in the writings of the Arizal and the Nefesh Hachaim, that through studying the holy Torah, a person can merit to extend the soul that he already has, adding another very holy soul, taken from an extremely high place. With this extension, he is able to change his entire spiritual condition for the good, literally from one extreme to the other. If so, any bad self evaluation of one's future strengths is erroneous since his assessment is based on the soul that he has already, without calculating that he could acquire more for his soul, which would change his entire situation.

5.

The Maharchav elaborates on this in the name of

Closeness to Hashem

the Arizal. He speaks about how forgetfulness weakens the Torah learning that one has already worked on. One forgets one's learning and therefore doesn't feel that he has gained anything by the learning. The Maharchav writes in the name of the Arizal, "This is incorrect because, in the future a person will remember everything that he ever learnt. Included in these words are two types of arguments against the excuse to lessen one's learning because of the likelihood to forget it. (1) Even if he will forget, it is only temporarily forgotten, and he will benefit from this learning forever, since he will remember it in the world to come. (2) The point of remembering it in the world to come isn't simply as a reward or a gift for his hard work, rather it is because the moment a person learns Torah, the radiance of that piece of Torah joins with the light in his own soul, and become eternally united. This already causes a person to remember his studies forever, just there are layers which cover this light, and withhold the memory from him. In the world to come these layers fall away." It comes out from this that although a person may not remember what he has learnt in this world, it still has great significance. From the moment that he learnt the Torah, there are more lofty spiritual lights attached to his soul, greatly raising his spiritual level.

Closeness to Hashem

6.

The fact that success in Torah study comes to a person beyond all limited measure is something that has proven itself throughout the generations. Many of those who became world giants were not suited for Torah study right from the start. Some had little talent and some seemingly had opposing character traits to those of diligence. Even so many strengthened themselves and succeeded in becoming leaders of Torah Jewry. Of course one who has great talent or inclination towards diligence, and all the more so with a combination of the two, will likely to have abundant success in Torah, Hashem forbid that we minimize the value of these things. However even someone who does not have these attributes can accomplish a great deal. We see this in massechet Avot, "Whoever learns Torah in poverty will in the end study it in wealth." It is said in the name of the Maharal Diskin that this applies not only to monetary poverty but also to deficiency in talent, where despite all a person strengthens himself to learn Torah. He will merit a wealth of abilities. [Far be it from us to belittle talents. Of course a person blessed with prodigious talents must take care to utilize them for Torah, as we see with the Maharil Diskin himself who from a young age, although blessed with great genius worked and toiled with incredible diligence in Torah, indeed quite

Closeness to Hashem

incomprehensibly, and as is well known merited to levels in genius which were beyond all laws of nature.]

Chapter Nine

The Words of the Bach (Ohr Hachaim 47) on the Mitzvah of Torah Study

1.
In massechet Nedarim, R' Yehuda and R' Mai say, "Who is the man who is wise and will understand this? And (with whom will) the word of Hashem will speak to him and tell him why the land was destroyed? This matter was asked of the wise men and the prophets and of the heavenly angels yet they could not explain it, until Hashem Himself explained it, as it says, 'and Hashem said, "For deserting My Torah which I put before them and they didn't hearken to My voice and they didn't follow it"'". What does it mean "…they didn't hearken to My voice and they didn't follow it"? R' Yehuda and Rav said, "Because they didn't bless the Torah first".

Closeness to Hashem

2.
The Bach in Ohr Hachaim (47) writes about this (slightly adapted). There is a great difficulty here. Why did He punish them so terribly severely for not blessing first, which seems to be a minor aveirah?

3.
He explains that Hashem's intention seems to be that we busy ourselves with Torah in order to reinforce our souls with strength, spirituality and the sanctity of the source of Torah. Hashem therefore gave His Torah of Truth to Yisrael as a gift, so that it not be forgotten from us, and so that our souls and our bodies with two hundred and forty eight limbs and our three hundred and sixty five sinews cling to the two hundred and forty eight positive mitzvot and the three hundred and sixty five negative mitzvot in the Torah. Had they had this intention whilst being busy with Torah, they themselves would have been the carriage and the palace of the presence of Hashem. The presence would have literally been within them. They themselves would have been the palaces of Hashem, Hashem's presence would have fixed its place of residence within them, and the land would have been illuminated with His glory. Through this the heavenly and earthly abodes would have been joined and become one single dwelling place.

Closeness to Hashem

4.

Now the judgment was passed. They had busied themselves only with the physical words of Torah. They had learnt Torah only so that the judges be able to use them in business matters, and used for the wise men to teach, neither intending to strengthen themselves nor to cling to the sanctity and spirituality of the Torah, nor to perpetuate the presence of Hashem here on Earth, nor so that their souls rise up to a high level after their death. With this they brought about the separation and departure of Hashem's presence from the land, and it rose up to heaven. The land was then left merely physical, devoid of holiness. This then caused its destruction and desolation.

5.

This is what Chazal meant, "Who is the person who is wise etc. for what reason was the land destroyed etc. and Hashem said, 'Because they abandoned my Torah which I have placed before them…' and He said, 'My Torah is a Torah of truth which I gave as a present. They shouldn't learn it and then forget it. I explained to them the reasons for everything and their explanations, and this is what I put before them like a laid table…'", which explains the verse, "And these are the laws which you should put before them." This means that they should connect to the essence of the sanctity of the Torah, the Torah of truth and in that

Closeness to Hashem

way Hashem's presence would reside amongst them. But they abandoned Torah and did not follow it. A journey in Torah spirituality, trying to move from level to level, is in order that the soul joins to the essence of the sanctity of the Torah. The generation at time of the destruction of the first temple did not follow it, meaning that when the time came to study Torah and to bless Hashem and praise Him for giving the Torah to His Jewish people, they didn't do it entirely for the sake of heaven, in order that their holiness join with His presence. This means that they didn't concentrate sufficiently on the blessing, "Who has chosen us from amongst all the nations", to think how Hashem brought us to Mt. Sinai and gave us His holy Torah, His beloved plaything with which He plays every day, so that our souls join with the holy essence of the Torah and it's spirituality and to bring down Hashem's presence amongst us. They didn't follow it in order to be busy with Torah for its own sake, and were therefore punished. The manifestation of Hashem moved away from them and the land was destroyed and left like a desert with no wayfarers passing by. This shows just how it was completely ruined and left as a piece of physicality. The holiness of Hashem's presence didn't pass by there any more because Hashem's presence had completely left the country and risen up heavenward. (Bach).

Closeness to Hashem

6.
To understand well the words of the Bach it is worthwhile to look at what is spoken about in chapter 2 on the saying, "The Holy One Blessed Be He and the Torah and Yisrael are all one". With that we can explain the words of the Bach on the topic of Torah study. Through Torah study, the lights of the soul couple with the lights of the holy Torah. As a result of this an outpouring of illumination from Hashem Himself pours into the soul.

7.
The Bach does not intend to add anything here to the basic explanation of Torah study, rather he comes to explain that this is the fundamental principle of the mitzvah of Torah study, and that through it a person connects with Hashem and brings light from Hashem Himself to his soul. As the Bach says, this is the main reason for the giving of the Torah to Yisrael. Therefore, when this was missing, automatically the land was destroyed and the nation exiled from it.

8.
It is extremely important that a person become used to this idea and to engrave it in his soul. In that way, every time he comes to busy himself with Torah, he will be connecting with the Creator Himself, linking up with Him, thereby receiving the powerful and holy outpouring of spiritual

Closeness to Hashem

bounty from the Creator of the world.

Chapter Ten

Any Torah Study and Mitzvah Performance Joins the Soul with His Creator and Brings a Spiritual and Holy Bounty from Hashem

An Answer for Those Who Claim They Don't Feel This

1.
It is written in numerous places in this work how for bit of Torah that a person learns, and through every mitzvah that a person performs, a spiritual bounty is created and pours from Hashem to the person's soul, sanctifying it and linking it to the Creator Himself. [The opposite is brought about, Hashem forbid, with an aveirah.]
2.
There are those who claim that they don't feel this

Closeness to Hashem

at all, or at least not keenly enough, especially when referring to a short amount of study etc.

3.

The truth is however, that with every small amount of study or mitzvah performance, there is a powerful outpouring of bounty. Hashem however created the world in a way that in this world the body is like a screen which blocks the soul from feeling any changes in it. [Not everyone is equal in respect to this screen, for some the barrier is greater and for some it is less, no place here for further elaboration]. The reason for this is so that the world be a world of challenges as the Mesillat Yesharim details in the first chapter. Were we to significantly feel the influence of mitzvot and aveirot on the soul, the existence of a test or challenge would be almost impossible?

4.

Only after a hundred and twenty years, when there is no longer the obstruction of the soul by the body, then a person will see the reality of how every moment of Torah study and every part of mitzvah performance brought intense light to his soul. This light does not just appear at the time when he sees it in heaven; rather it is then that he sees how the light had already come at the actual time of the learning and the mitzvah performance. Indeed, the strength of these very lights enabled and assisted him to achieve many things in this

Closeness to Hashem

world. It was just the screen that prevented him from seeing reality. Many times, one can actually feel the good resulting from this strength but doesn't realize to connect it to the Torah that he learned or the mitzvah that he did.

5.

This can be compared to a person undergoing an operation under the effects of general anesthesia, and the surgeon asks him at the end of the operation if he can cut a further few more cm deeper than necessary. If the patient is a fool he will agree since he anyway can't feel anything now due to the strength of the general anesthetic. However, if he is a clever person, he will refuse this since even though now he cannot feel anything, he knows that when he awakens from the anesthesia every extra cm cut will hurt tremendously. Were they to cut him when he was anaesthetized, then when he comes around he will see that the incision was made at the time when they cut him and not when he woke up. It is exactly the same with aveirot and mitzvot. Of course, many times a person merits this elevated feeling from mitzvot already in this world. [This is non comparable to the natural feeling of satisfaction that comes when a person does something that he thinks to be correct - see 'Chayei Olam' from the Kehilot Yaacov.]

Closeness to Hashem

Chapter Eleven

Mitzvot Between Man and His Fellow

1.
Mitzvot between man and his fellow are of the basics of Judaism. This means to endeavor to benefit another, and to take care not to cause suffering to one's fellow, as it says in the gemarah in massechet Yevamot that mercifulness and loving kindnesses are the purpose of Yisreal - see inside for further detail.

2.
Although it is obvious that every Jew wants to benefit his fellow, and not cause him any harm, there are two errors often made in this area, causing many to stumble. The first is that many times when a person tries to do something good for his friend but doesn't succeed, he thinks that it was a waste of time and he is discouraged from continuing to do similar acts in the future.

3.

Closeness to Hashem

This is a terrible mistake, proven by Avraham Avinu who put himself out so much to feed the angels, as is detailed in parshat Vayiera, and it is clear from the gemarah in Bava Metziah - chapter 7 - that in this merit when his children, the Yisraelites were in the desert for forty years, manna fell down for them, as well as many other things. This means that he received tremendous reward for his deeds; millions of people were fed miraculously with food from heaven every day for forty years! [This wasn't even the entire reward - there was even more than this.] Yet when Avraham gave the angels to eat, in the simplest way to understand it, he wasn't really benefiting them, since angels don't need to eat. But he didn't know that they were angels and therefore fed them. Through this test of giving to another he received such a huge reward.

4.

The explanation why there is such a great reward for trying to help another person, even if he didn't succeed in benefiting him in the end, could be because he has the good will, and acts as a result of his desire to do good. The Chafetz Chaim says however, that there is an even greater additional point here, as we explained above, that the way the world runs is that whatever happens in the higher worlds is according to our behavior in this world, and according to what happens in the higher

Closeness to Hashem

worlds there are results in this world. The Chafetz Chaim explains that whenever a Jew tries to do an act of kindness in this world, whether he succeeds in the matter or not, he awakens the attributes of kindness in the higher worlds, thereby bringing great goodness to the entire Jewish nation. It therefore follows that it is not possible that a person tries to do kindness but didn't achieve anything; rather, whenever a person tries to perform loving kindnesses, he always brings kindnesses to other areas through awakening the attributes of kindness in the higher worlds.

5.

At any rate, as the Chafetz Chaim brings from Chazal, that when a person does perform the kindness and does benefit another, the mitzvah and the reward is much much greater.

6.

The second oft mistaken point in the area of the will to help and to hold back from hurting others, is that people think it refers only to big things and not small ones, for example there people who are very careful not to hurt others in a big way, but aren't so careful not to hurt others in a small way, whereas in truth one needs to take care not to hurt others even in a very small way. The Chazon Ish writes in his collection of letters, that to hurt someone with words, even slightly and even for a short amount of time, is a Torah prohibition. This

Closeness to Hashem

is something very difficult to take care in, but it is really a great obligation upon every person to try hard to do. Praiseworthy is the one who manages to be entirely vigilant in this area.

7.
As a result of this, when it comes to helping others, it need not be just in big matters. It is a mitzvah to do so in small matters too.

8.
A further important principle in this area is how very careful a person always has to be. Often when one is in a desperate, yet oft occurring situation, it is not always noticed by the world around him, but within his heart this person is broken to pieces. Someone who insults such a person, even very slightly, can greatly pain him, because it joins with the terrible pain already within him. The same is true of the opposite. One who merits gladdening such a person, even in a small way, can really transform the way he feels.

9.
On a similar vein, there is a story of a person who came to ask the Chazon Ish advice about some every day issues, some very petty matters. It was simply hard for this person to make decisions by himself, and all his doubts weighed heavily upon him. The Chazon Ish answered every single question. When the person apologized to the Chazon Ish for taking his time from important

Closeness to Hashem

things for such insignificant matters, the Chazon Ish replied that even people who come to ask him about important worldly things, like purchasing a home etc. what he does for them is not the decision that he makes for them, rather the main help is that he puts their minds at rest through his advice. If so, then there really is no difference between them and this person who to calm his mind needed help deciding petty matters. From here we learn a fundamental principle. The mitzvah to help others and to refrain from hurting them applies even to small things. Even more than this, often small things are not small things at all, but really big matters, since in that particular area they can bring great pain or great happiness.

10.
The area of mitzvot between man and his fellow also applies to matters of spirituality. It is a tremendous mitzvah to help someone who is spiritually needy. When someone knows that his friend doesn't understand a part of the gemarah well and requires help, it is a great mitzvah to help him. It is clear from Chazal that through this the helper himself will also merit great success in his studies.

11.
Furthermore, there is the point explained earlier, that every time that a Jew learns Torah or performs

Closeness to Hashem

a mitzvah, he helps the entire Jewish nation. Through his Torah study or mitzvah performance the upper worlds are established and bounties of goodness and spiritual and physical blessings come down to the Jewish nation. This is especially when a person for some reason finds it hard to learn, and he could choose to stop learning, yet he takes hold of himself and continues further because he has mercy on those suffering and wants to help them with his learning. This is definitely considered a very great mitzvah between man and his fellow. [Obviously every mitzvah between man and his fellow is also between man and Hashem too, since Hashem commanded that he do it.]

Closeness to Hashem

Chapter Twelve

The Greatness Acquired Through Torah Study

Part 1

A major feature of Torah study is that every word one studies, one fulfils a positive mitzvah and merits awesome reward.

1.
In the book 'Shenot Eliyahu' of the Vilna Gaon [which is an explanation to the mishnayot, printed in at the back of some editions] on massechet Peah (81:41) Chazal write, "A person must love the Torah very much, since every word that he learns is a mitzvah on it's own. If so then after learning one page, for example, he fulfils many hundreds

Closeness to Hashem

of mitzvot." The Chafetz Chaim brings these words in his book 'Shem Olam', sha'ar Hachzakat HaTorah chapter 9 (11:4).

2.

The Chafetz Chaim writes further, following along the same lines, that with every word that a person learns, an angel is created who advocates on his behalf.

3.

In the Yerushalmi (4a) there we find, "Rebi Berachia, Rebi Chiya of C'far Dechumin [Rebi Chiya was from a place called C'far Dechumin], (were sitting) one said, "Even the entire world cannot be compared to one word of Torah." We see that if one were offered all the silver and gold and precious things and high positions in the world, or to give all that up in order to learn just one word of Torah, it is more worthwhile for him to choose the one word of Torah, since by learning one word of Torah he earns himself world to come, more enjoyable and worth thousands and thousands of times more than anything in this world. [Someone on a higher spiritual level will feel that performing Hashem's will and the resulting closeness to Hashem that comes with Torah study is worth more to him than anything in this world.] In addition, the Yerushalmi refer to one word of Torah study, how much more so when a person regularly busies himself with Torah, each

Closeness to Hashem

time learning many words of Torah.

4.

Here we see many things to awaken us to study Torah. The first is that when a person decides how to settle his future, he should be aware of the huge profit he could gain were he to secure Torah study in his future. Secondly, even a person who is constantly engaged in Torah, or in the opposite extreme, someone whose life situation excludes the possibility that Torah study be the main activity, and he has a small amount of free time, he should muster all his strength to use this time for Torah. If one uses even his shortest spare moments in this way, he will earn multitudes of mitzvot, each one huge and powerful, as we know is the magnitude of the mitzvah performance of Torah study.

Closeness to Hashem

Part 2

How the Torah study of the Jewish nation is the purpose of creating the world.

1.
The Chafetz Chaim writes in his book 'Shem Olam', sha'ar Hachzokat HaTorah, chapter 9, [slightly adapted], "Behold it is well known that the study of Torah is a positive Torah mitzvah, as the verse says, 'And you should teach them and keep them do to them." The creation of man was principally in order that he toil in Torah, as the gemarah Sanhedrin writes in chapter Chelek (99) "A person was created to toil, as the verse says, 'A person was born to labour' ; this is the labour of Torah, as the verse says, "This Torah scroll must never move from your mouths.".".
2.
See further in the Nefesh Hachaim, sha'ar 4, chapter 13 for a lengthier discussion on the subject.
3.
The true desire of every Jew is to bring pleasure to his Creator. The more a person acknowledges that the main reason for creating the world is for the

Closeness to Hashem

study of Torah, it is then implicit that out of the desire to bring pleasure to his Creator, he will increase his Torah study.

4.

Since the main reason why the world was created was for the study of Torah, it is clear that this is the great bringer of closeness to Hashem. A person has a great desire to be close to Hashem and to receive reward in the Gan Eden. When one fulfils Hashem's will in order to come close to Hashem, this is the great reward bringer in the world to come.

5.

Although it is now understood that Torah learning is the main reason for creating the world, one must learn and also try to keep the Torah. One cannot Hashem forbid, cast off the yoke of performance, saying that if Torah study is the main reason for the creation of the world, he will do just that and not do mitzvoth. Such learning will not justify creating the world. See the book 'Ana Avda' which brings, in the name of the Chazon Ish, that the main purpose of a person in this world is to live in holiness, in areas of the attribute of Yesod. The way to come to this is through Torah study. There is no contradiction here; it is all the same point. Should a person Hashem forbid find himself in a spiraling spiritual descent, it should not prevent him from studying Torah, quite the

Closeness to Hashem

opposite, he should strengthen himself with all his might in Torah study, and this will help him to get out of this difficulty and to speedily return and be close to Hashem.

Closeness to Hashem

Part 3

How Torah study changes a person's essence.

1.
In the introduction to the Zohar (p.12) and also in the Nefesh Hachaim (sha'ar 4, chapter 15) [in the translated version] we find that, "It is a mitzvah to be engaged in the study of Torah and to try hard every day in the study of Torah, since a person who learns Torah, his soul acquires another holy soul and becomes like a holy angel." This is a tremendous encouragement for a person to muster all his strength in the area of Torah study, since every Jew wants to climb higher and become close to Hashem, to be more spiritual and purer, to change his very being for one more holy. Were one to discover a way that was guaranteed to achieve this one would be prepared to invest huge amounts for this; in which case the gates are open wide for such a person, as brought here at the beginning of this topic. There is in fact a guaranteed way to get there, and that is to increase one's study of the holy Torah. Torah study will purify his soul and he will rise and climb in levels of closeness to Hashem. That is the true purity and

Closeness to Hashem

the true elevation.

2.

There are people who find it hard to awaken themselves to this since the change in the person brought about by Torah study is not recognizable. It appears that he is in a period where he is only investing in Torah, like the period beforehand.

3.

A person must therefore get himself used to seeing his situation according to the spiritual truth and not by what it physically appears to be. It is written in the book of the Chazon Ish 'Emunah and Bitachon' that a person can be on a level close to that of an angel and yet still mix with others, who don't notice any difference between him and themselves. The truth is only according to what lies inside the person. This is brought clearly from all the Rishonim when they speak about prophecy. This is such an awesomely high level we cannot even describe it. And yet we see in the book of Melachim when the Shunamit spoke to Elisha, she saids, "Behold I know that a man…holiness passes over us". The gemarah asks how she knew this. They explain that she saw that there were never any flies near to his table, meaning that without this proof it would have been impossible to know that he was a holy person even though he was on an incredibly high level!

4.

Closeness to Hashem

The point of this here is not to tell a person that he is obligated to hide his actions in a way that nothing of his high level be seen outside, although this is correct behaviour as the verse says, "Walk with modesty...", it is indeed a very great thing. It is brought in the Chovat Halvavot that there is a great danger when a person behaves in the same way as everybody else in order to secret his own spiritual level. In reality this will cause him to greatly minimize his service of Hashem, for example he will pray more shortly than how he would really like to pray, without swallowing the words, and the same will happen in many other areas too. The Chovot Halvavot writes that as a result of this a person can fall from all his high levels. A person must therefore be very careful not to hide himself. In any case the intention of the words here is to say that many times a person will behave in an elevated manner for a time and yet when contemplating whether to continue with it, or to move on to higher levels, he decides against it since he reasons that it is not worth the effort it takes to grow, since one anyway does not see a great difference from the growth. The words written above come to rebuff this mistake, as the truth is that it is very likely that through this elevation his spiritual level rose thousands more times than what it was previously, even though it is not recognizable to the outside world.

Closeness to Hashem

5.
There is however a greater problem than that mentioned above. Many times, the barrier to awaken oneself to study Torah is not just that the change is not recognizable, but that one cannot feel the change at all within himself.

6.
However, it is important to know the truth. Whoever dedicates himself to learn Torah, his inner self automatically changes to become holier and purer. If he doesn't feel this it is only because there is a screen on the body preventing him from feeling this - as explained at length above in chapter 10.

Closeness to Hashem

Part 4

Further changes to the inner person due to Torah study.

1.
The Chafetz Chaim writes that if a person were to take the skin of an animal, which is a regular item, not containing any holiness at all, and tans it with the intention that it be used for a Torah scroll, and writes a Torah scroll on it, this skin becomes holy with an awesome holiness, a Torah scroll greatness that is well known. How much more so when a person takes his brain and tells it words of Torah! It is certain that his brain contents will be sanctified with tremendous holiness. In a Torah scroll it is merely written on top of the parchment whereas in the brain the Torah enters inside the brain. The difference between a person before he has learnt Torah and after he has learnt Torah is like the difference between the regular piece of skin and the Torah scroll which is sacred and with tremendous sanctity.

2.
In truth every Jew, even without having learnt Torah still has a great amount of holiness within

Closeness to Hashem

him just because he is a Jew. The Chafetz Chaim adds here the difference between the sanctity of a Jew before he learns Torah and the sanctity of a Jew after he has learnt Torah, the difference is enormous, like that of the regular skin and the very holy Torah scroll.

3.

Accordingly, even a person who has already learnt much Torah, still, when he learns for an additional amount of time, his essence is exchanged for an even holier one, just like the ordinary skin becomes the holy Torah scroll.

Closeness to Hashem

Part 5

One who is busy with Torah merits special supernatural heavenly help.

1.
The Nefesh Hachaim (sha'ar 4: chapter 18) writes that one who accepts the yoke of the holy Torah upon himself, honestly and for its own sake, he is raised above everything in this world and Hashem attends to him with individual attention, way above all the natural forces. This is because he is joined to the Torah and therefore to The Holy One Blessed Be He, so to speak. He is sanctified with the lofty sanctity of the holy Torah, which is more valuable than anything of value in any of the worlds. It is the Torah which gives vitality and permanence to all the worlds and all the forces of nature. It follows therefore that a person who busies himself with Torah brings life and stability to everything and is superior to everything. How can it then be that such a person's attendance from Hashem be via natural powers?!

2.
This means that one who busies himself with Torah for its own sake merits heavenly assistance

Closeness to Hashem

in his affairs, way above what is natural. It is even possible that those around him don't sense this. Supernatural things can still come in a hidden way; the viewer can still err and think that it is all natural. However, the reality that he receives is unbelievable; the very individual care from heaven. Fortunate is he who merits this.

3.

Although this is written about one who learns Torah for its own sake and not about anyone who learns Torah, it need not weaken a person's inspiration to learn Torah. The Nefesh Hachaim writes clearly about this, as explained earlier, exactly what 'for its own sake' means. He writes (sha'ar 4: chapter 3) that 'Torah for its own sake' does not mean incredible closeness to Hashem and great levels of spirituality which many find hard to acquire, rather it means to learn in order to understand the holy Torah and not for any other physical, worldly objectives, for example to receive honor or to enjoy a quarrel etc. Many merits achieving learning with the simple intention to get to know Torah and understand it. This is Torah for its own sake. One may not always manage this, but at least a large part of one's studies can certainly be with the simple intention to know the Torah and understand it.

4.

Even though the Nefesh Hachaim has already

Closeness to Hashem

explained what is considered as Torah for its own sake, still it is definitely true that it is a higher level when a person concentrates in his learning to bring pleasure to his Creator, more and more, resulting in his learning being with more of a feeling of closeness to Hashem. In addition, the actual learning that he did is also reckoned on a higher level. Although the Nefesh Hachaim (sha'ar 3) writes that closeness to Torah is automatically closeness to Hashem since the Torah is the word of Hashem, there are nevertheless many levels to this. The Nefesh Hachaim hints to this (sha'ar 3) after having lengthily explained all the different types of service of Hashem and closeness to Him. He writes there (chapter 14) that the highest of all types of closeness to Hashem is when one achieves really fearing Hashem, to be fulfilled at least during prayer, or at least for some time during prayer. He writes there (chapter 14, towards the end of the brackets) that at the time of engaging in Torah it is very great to have intention to have this fear. At any rate, it is clear from the Nefesh Hachaim high levels of spirituality are not required in order to merit all that one can merit through learning Torah for its own sake, i.e. receiving supernatural divine assistance. The basic level of 'Torah for its own sake' is that one's objective not be for worldly things, rather his aim should be to know and to comprehend Torah.

Closeness to Hashem

5.

It will certainly not be detrimental if one adds some thoughts of holiness to the basic level of 'for its own sake'. In fact, quite the opposite; it is a bonus. An example of these thoughts could be to intend to bring pleasure to Hashem, or to increase the merits of the Jewish nation and bring salvation to the Jewish nation, or in order to teach it to others, (his intention to teach others should be for their good and not to be haughty), or he thinks that he wants to know how to perform the mitzvoth better. Good intentions certainly add and not detract as we see in the mishna in masechet Avot, "He who learns in order to teach or to do is preferable than one who just learns."

Closeness to Hashem

Chapter Thirteen

Sacrifice for Torah study and Surrender of Things Which Prevents Vigilance in Torah study

1.
The gemarah in massechet Brachot (71b) says, "Once the wicked ruling kingdom decreed that Yisrael may not involve themselves with Torah. Rebi Akiva came, gathered groups of people and publicly taught them Torah... it was but a few days later that they caught Rebi Akiva and imprisoned him. When they brought out Rebi Akiva to kill him it was the time for the reading of the Shema. As they were combing his flesh with iron combs, he was accepting the yoke of heaven upon himself. His disciples said to him, 'Our teacher, even now?' he replied, 'All my life I was troubled by the verse in shema, "(Love Hashem)

Closeness to Hashem

with all your life, which means even if they take your life", I always asked myself, "When will the opportunity come my way to fulfil this?" Now that it has come my way should I not fulfil it? …' (See text inside for the entire happening)."

2.

The gemarah in masechet Sanhedrin (13b and 14a) says, "Reb Yehuda and Rav Baram said, 'Remember that man for good; his name is Rebi Yehuda Ben Baba, if not for him the laws of fines would have been forgotten and anulled from Yisrael. [to pass judgement on fines one needs a rav with semicha and the gentiles had decreed against giving semicha - see further.] Once the wicked kingdom decreed against Yisrael that anyone who gives semicha would be killed and whoever would receive semicha would be killed … what did Rebi Yehuda Ben Baba do? … he gave semicha …to five elders; Rebi Meir, Rebi Yehuda [Bar Iloy], Rebi Shimon [Bar Yochai], Rebi Yosi [Bar Chalafta] and Rebi Elozor Ben Shamua. Rav Avyah also added Reb Nechemia. When their enemies came to know about these. He said to them, [Rebi Yehuda Ben Baba to his disciples] 'My children, run!'. They said to him, 'Rebi what will become of you?' He replied, 'Behold I am cast before them like a stone which will not be overturned.' They said to him, [the gentiles] 'Move from there! Until they stabbed

Closeness to Hashem

him with three hundred iron spears and made him like a sieve. [Meaning that they gave him a terrible death]."

3.

The gemarah in massechet Avodah Zarah (18:1) explains that at the time when the gentiles decreed forbidding Torah study, Rebi Chanina Ben Tradyon was still busy learning Torah and gathering groups in public to learn Torah whilst holding a Torah scroll against his chest. The gentiles came along and burned him.

4.

Even though generally to save a persons life takes priority over most other things, however at a time of a decree against performing mitzvot the law is different. Look carefully at Yoreh Deah (127) for details on this topic, when saving a life takes precedence and when not, there is no place to elaborate further.

5.

In any case, we see from all these extracts that our teachers, the Tanaim gave up their lives for the mitzvah of teaching Torah to the congregation. We see from this the magnitude of the importance of Torah study, and how a person is commanded to give up on so many things if they are at the expense of his Torah study. If world leaders gave up their very lives in order to teach Torah, surely there are many things that we can surrender order

Closeness to Hashem

to study Torah.

6.

In massechet Shabbat (83b) we see, "Raish Lokish said, 'The words of Torah find permanence only in one who kills himself over them, as the verse says, "This is the law when a person dies in a tent". It is obvious here that the intention here is not that a person kill himself in order to learn Torah, since if he would be dead, how could he learn?! More than that, the mitzvah of preserving a human life is more important. [The examples brought above were at a time of decree, as mentioned there.] Instead the intention of the gemarah with these stories is to show that there are very many things which are precious to a person, like for example if a person has a very strong leaning to a certain profession, or a very great desire to become monetarily wealthy, and he feels in his heart that it is so hard for him to give up on his desires, as if he were nearly to die because of it. This is exactly what the gemarah speaks about here, that the true way to acquire Torah is to forgo these desires in order to learn Torah. This is the way to attain Torah. The above examples of desires are of things which touch very much on the future of a person. The same also applies to smaller things. If someone is in doubt how to spend the next few hours, whether to spend the time learning Torah or to go and converse about an incident that

Closeness to Hashem

happened which very much interests him, or any other thing which will waste his time from learning, he may feel that it is very hard for him to give up this thing. Here lays the mitzvah mentioned in the gemarah, that by breaking this desire and going to learn, against his own strong will, he suffers a partial aspect of death, he kills that desire. This is one of the acquisitions of Torah.

7.

The gemarah implies more here. In reality Torah study necessitates a person to forgo even his most basic necessities. We see this in massechet Avot, "That is the way of the Torah, you eat bread and salt and you drink a set measure of water, you sleep on the floor and you labor in Torah. If you do so, you are fortunate and it is good for you. You are fortunate in this world and it will be good for you in the next world." The reality is however that it is not generally necessary to sacrifice one's absolute bare necessities in order to learn Torah. We therefore brought present day examples which are more widespread nowadays. These are also included in the intention of the gemarah. Still a person still has to know that if Hashem forbid, things turn around, and a test comes, in order to learn Torah, he may have to forgo even basic necessities. He may even have to live in the very restricted way, described in the mishna in

Closeness to Hashem

massechet Avot. He should strengthen himself to stand as firm as a flint stone and as an iron pillar and not to abandon Torah, as Chazal say, "One (thing achieved) with difficulty is better than a hundred without difficulty."

8.

The gemarah Shabbat (83b) says further, "R' Yonatan would say, 'A person should never hold himself back from going to the Bet Midrash or from learning words of Torah, even at the time of one's death, as the verse says, "This is the law of a person who dies in a tent", even at the time of death one should be busy with Torah." In general, a person's challenge in Torah study is not at the time of his death, rather whilst he is still alive. Of course, from the words of the gemarah regarding death one must take a lesson for the many hours which could be used for Torah study. Sometimes it is difficult for a person to imagine using his free time for Torah, and it can be a very remote idea to spend spare hours in the Bet Midrash, either because of his personal situation, or because of the individual details of that particular time. Nevertheless from the words of the gemarah we see that one is still obligated to learn; since if even at the time of death a person should not hold himself back from going to the Bet Midrash and from busying himself with Torah, how much more so all the times when a person has minor

Closeness to Hashem

hindrances from learning, they are obviously of a much lesser degree.

Closeness to Hashem

Chapter Fourteen

Prayer

Part one

Awakening to the importance of prayer and it's details.

1.
In the gemarah in Brachot (6b) it says, "One of the Rabbis said to R' Bayvo Bar Abaye, and some say that it was R' Bayvo to R' Nachman Bar Yitzchok, 'What thing is very elevated and yet degraded by people?' [Meaning that it says this in Tehillim (12) and they asked how to understand the verse]. He told them, 'The thing which stands at the pinnacle of the world and people degrade it." Rashi explains, "Things that stand at the top of the world mean prayer which rises upwards." The

Closeness to Hashem

evaluation that many give prayer is usually much less than it's actual worth. Accordingly, it is fitting that a person to make the effort to elevate his personal evaluation of prayer, to bring it somewhat closer to its true worth. One of the ways to achieve this is to learn about the essence of prayer. We will bring here - please Hashem - a sampling of what there is to understand on this.

2.
In truth, there is much to say about the commandment of prayer. Prayer is divided into praises, requests and thanks. As we see in the gemarah in Brachot 34b about the shemone esreh prayer, "R' Chanina said, 'The first ones [meaning the first brachot of the shemone esreh] are compared to a servant who offers praises before his master, the middle ones are compared to a servant who requests a reward from his master, and the last ones are compared to a servant who just received a reward from his master, thanks him and leaves and goes away."

3.
There is another definition of prayer in the context of it being a service of the heart. There is the sensation of closeness to Hashem and there is the begging of one's Creator to do him a personal favor and give him the good things that he requests. Prayers which are requests are extremely powerful. The actual asking creates the correct

Closeness to Hashem

feelings in a person's mind, that all that he has comes only from Hashem Himself and there is no other means to get what he needs from Him. [I have not explained at depth whether there are further areas in prayer, I have written in a generalized manner.]

Closeness to Hashem

Part 2

The clinging of one's thoughts to Hashem, during prayer and at all other times.

1.
We will explain a little about the joining of thoughts with Hashem. Joining one's thoughts to Hashem is a very great mitzvah. This is clear from the Rishonim and Acharonim, the main mitzvah not being especially during prayer. On a high level, a person would have his thoughts joined to Hashem at every moment. Many Rishonim and Acharonim explain this, see the Nefesh Hachaim (sha'ar 3: chapters 13 and 14) where he writes about the holy Avot and about Moshe Rabbeinu who, without a moments break, had their thoughts united with their Creator, throughout their lives - see the Nefesh Hachaim for many more details on this.

2.
Of course, even someone who cannot manage this high level should still try what he can. For most people, the most successful time to do this is

Closeness to Hashem

during prayers. If he cannot always manage this he should at least try partially. How much one can achieve this is very much dependant on the soul roots of a person and on the individual details of his personal situation. In any case, even one who cannot manage this should still not despair, for even without this he can merit to high levels in service of Hashem. What is almost certain is that even if he cannot do this at present, there will be other times when he will be able to achieve this. The principle here is that every situation which is sent to a person from heaven, even though it seems to him that it is a very difficult situation in which to serve Hashem, he can strengthen himself with all his might to serve Hashem with great and awesome servitude.

3.

When it comes to being close to Hashem there are those who err and think that it is just a sensation of the heart and nothing more. This is not true. Even though it is expressed as a feeling of being close to Hashem in one's heart, in truth there is much more to it than this. This is explained in Rishonim and Acharonim [see the book 'Sha'arei Kedushah' of our teacher, Harav Chaim Vital (3:5)] that through a person joining his thoughts to his Creator, he is actually adding in a very real way to his connection with the Creator of the world, strengthening his soul's link with Him.

Closeness to Hashem

Additional outpourings from the radiance of Hashem's face descend to one who attaches himself to his Creator.

4.

It is difficult to extend here with a detailed explanation on exactly how this works, since it is connected to so many Kabbalistic ideas. Still the general idea remains from that which is explained in Rishonim and Acharonim. Just as it is possible to join two physical items together in this world through certain actions e.g. two boards by hammering and nailing them together, it is also possible to join the soul in a certain way to The Creator Himself. The particular action which brings about this join is the one which links a person's thoughts with his Creator. Although we have no grasp at all of the essence of Hashem, we can still explain that through this connection, Hashem will bring a holy spiritual outpouring to the soul of the one who joins his thoughts to his Creator. It follows, that the joining of thoughts to Hashem and the firing of one's thoughts to the causes of Hashem is not just intellectual or just emotional; it is a reality. When a person thinks about Hashem this he really changes to be more connected to the Creator of the world with a very real spiritual connection.

5.

Even though this connection is spiritual and a very

Closeness to Hashem

real existence. It can be compared to angels who are spiritual but cannot be touched, still they most definitely exist.

6.

It is obviously that even without this closeness, the soul of every Jew is very much joined to his Creator and benefits from the radiance of His face. All that is written here that it this closeness is produced by a person thinking of his Creator, means that it strengthens the connection and adds to it.

7.

In truth, every mitzvah and every Torah learning improve the bond of the soul with it's Creator, as explained above. At times when a person doesn't feel this [the lack of this feeling is explained at length in chapter 10], then the joining of thoughts discussed here is a certain type of linking with Hashem which definitely brings this feeling and has a unique spiritual advantage over connections which one does not feel. This is not necessarily more important; every area and for every mitzvah in the service of Hashem has its own special advantages.

Closeness to Hashem

Part 3

More on the unification of one's thoughts with Hashem

1.
It is important to know that many find it very difficult to hear big demands in their search for closeness to Hashem. It is necessary simply to pray and to try to concentrate on the meaning of the words. The closeness will then come by itself. In any case it is important to know the greatness of the attribute of being close to Hashem, in order that a person concentrates more on the meaning of the words of prayer. This will help him to achieve closeness to Hashem. In addition, one who merits this closeness to Hashem should try as hard as possible not to lose it.

2.
The Ramchal writes in his book Adir Bamarom, that this unity of thoughts with Hashem atones for sins, meaning that the joining of the soul to the Creator cleans the soul from the dirt of sin. He does not mean to exempt the mitzvah of repentance, or to make light of doing sins for one who regularly experiences closeness to Hashem.

Closeness to Hashem

However, even when we are careful not to sin and do repent, still to our regret there is always much to correct. There is no place here to elaborate on this. One can however help himself by being close to Hashem.

3.

A person should know that the mitzvah of closeness to Hashem is very precious. Even if one merits to this just once a month or even less frequently, he should seize hold of what he can merit, with all his strength. Those who find it easier to achieve this closeness to Hashem, perhaps even experiencing it a few times a day, either during the prayer times or outside of prayer, should try all the more so in this area.

4.

The Nefesh Hachaim explains at length in sha'ar 4 how the unifying of one's thoughts with Hashem at the time of studying Torah is not necessary. This is because he is joined with the Torah study and is therefore automatically considered as being joined to Hashem, since Torah is the word of Hashem. See the text inside for further discussion on the matter. In any case, even though he agrees that there is no obligation in this area, still there is a higher level if a person can add thoughts of his Creator to his Torah learning - note well his words in sha'ar 3: chapter 14 near the end in brackets, and what is written above about this in chapter 12: part

Closeness to Hashem

5: point 4, there is no place to elaborate further here. In truth, there are those who find that the best way for them to achieve closeness to Hashem is through the study of the holy Torah. This raises their souls to link up with the Creator.

5.

See further what is written above in part 2: point 2 about this area for those who find it very hard to reach unifying their thoughts with Hashem.

Closeness to Hashem

Part 3

Requests in prayer and personal requests

1.
One of the fundamental principles in prayer is the knowledge that The Holy One Blessed Be He is merciful. He does favors, listens to the requests of those who beseech Him and helps them. It is clear in our holy writings that there is no prayer that returns empty-handed. Indeed, every Jew's appeal to Hashem activates salvations. Sometimes Hashem uses a person's request to produce a different salvation which is better suited to this person. Still it is an obligation to know and to believe that many times the salvation requested is indeed initiated.

2.
Every person must familiarize himself with the belief that everything that he wants and asks for is dependant only on The Holy One Blessed Be He. It is written that this is actually part of the mitzvah of requests in prayer which teaches that the matter is dependant only on Hashem. This is great service of Hashem and apart from this such a prayer will be accepted and delivered.

Closeness to Hashem

3.
It is very important that a person regularly asks for the things pertinent to him in a pleading manner. The more imploring the prayer, the more it is accepted [especially if one merits to beseech with tears as it says in the gemarah, "The gates of tears were never locked". We find in the anthology of letters of the Chazon Ish how he advises to approach prayer for success in Torah with tears, through contemplating with deep pain how little merits one has in Torah, until from the pain he comes to cry tears over it - see the letter itself - I don't have the book to hand at present].

4.
There are those who find it easier to appeal with emotion if he can word the request in his own way. This is permissible and correct according to halacha. One may add a request at the end of the Shemone Esreh before the last yiheyu lerotzon. A person may also ask Hashem for his needs, with whichever words he wants even not during prayer. [A person must take care not to request bad for another person even if he causes him pain. This is a very severe transgression; one should only pray for good things].

5.
Chazal speak in many places how the circumstances of the Jewish nation were very often changed for the better, all in the merit of the

Closeness to Hashem

prayers of individuals. The power of prayer is immense. In the anthology of letters of the Chazon Ish there is an expression saying, "Prayer is like a mighty stick in the hands of man to hugely improve his circumstances, through pleading about them to his Creator. His prayer will be accepted and his situation will greatly improve."

Closeness to Hashem

Chapter Fifteen

The Great Obligation to Be as Busy as Possible with the Holy Torah

1.
The Nefesh Hachaim writes in sha'ar 4: chapter 15 how we have been commanded from the mouth of Hashem Himself with an awesome warning, "This Torah scroll must never leave your mouth and you must toil in it day and night." [Joshua 1:8]. The Zohar writes in his introduction [the translated version], "Come and see just how mighty the power of Torah is, and how it is loftier than anything…" It is therefore necessary that a person put all his effort into Torah Day and night and not separate himself from the Torah. This is what it means when it is written, "And you should toil in it day and night". If one turns away from or separates himself from the Torah, it is as if he has cut himself off from the tree of life.

Closeness to Hashem

2.
The Tana Debei Eliyahu, Seder Eliyahu Zuta chapter 13, says that a person should put great effort into learning the words of Torah. The words of Torah are compared to bread and water, teaching us that just as it is impossible for a person to exist without bread and water so too he cannot exist without Torah, as the verse says, "This Torah scroll must never leave your mouth…" We find a similar idea in the medrash Tanchuma in parshat Ki Tsavo on the verse, "And it will be when you will surely listen…" We find this also in parshat Ha'azinu and in the medrash in Tehillim 1.

3.
The pasuk writes [Mishlei 3:18], "It is a tree of life for those who grasp it…" A person must entrench in his heart and imagine in his mind that were he drowning in a raging river and then saw a strong tree in front of him in the river, he would summon up the strength to seize the tree and cling to it with all his might. His hands wouldn't weaken from holding it for even a moment. His entire life depends on this tree. Who is foolish enough not to understand that if he is lazy, Hashem forbid, even for one moment, and his grip weakens, he will surely drown?

4.
So too the holy Torah is called the tree of life. Only when a person grasps this tree of life with

Closeness to Hashem

love, and is busy with it, regularly laboring over it, then he lives the real, upper life, connected and joined, so to speak, with the One who is eternally living, blessed be His name, since the Holy One Blessed Be He and Torah are one.

5.

Further, in chapter 34 of Tana Debei Eliyahy [adapted] he writes; "From the time of the destruction of our Holy Temple, and the children were exiled from their father's table, the Holy presence of Hashem and His glory wanders - so to speak - without respite. There is nothing left, only this Torah. When Yisrael, the holy nation, are busy with Torah as they should, they themselves are like a miniature sanctuary, to prepare for and to satisfy the Holy Presence, which will rest with them and spreads its wings over them, so to speak. Through this, Hashem has a little reprieve, as Chazal say in chapter 141 in Brachot (8a), "From the day that the Holy Temple was destroyed, the Holy One Blessed Be He has nothing in this world apart from the four amot of halacha".

6.

They continue and say, "How do we know that the holy presence of Hashem rests even on a lone person who sits and studies Torah? Since the verse says, 'In every place that I mention...'" The medrash in Mishlei at the end of chapter 8, explains the verse "Whoever finds me has found

Closeness to Hashem

life." Hashem says, "Anyone who is situated in the words of Torah, so too I am situated within him in every place." The verse therefore says, "Whoever finds me has found life."

7.

A sensible person will see and understand his way in holiness. He will seize his route, ready to be busy with Torah all the days of his life, and to despise evil and to choose that which is good for him and for all creations and worlds, to bring pleasure to his Former and Creator, blessed be His Name.

Closeness to Hashem

Chapter Sixteen

Mesillat Yesharim - Chapter 25

1.
In Mesillat Yesharim chapter 25, he writes how to acquire a high level of fear of Hashem. The way to acquire this awe is to contemplate two very true things. The first is that the Presence of Hashem exists in every place in the world and He himself watches over everything, small or big. Nothing is hidden from His eyes, neither due to it's magnitude, nor its lowliness. Rather every big thing and every small thing, every minor thing and every major thing, He, without distinction sees and understands.

2.
That is what is written [Yishiah 6:3], "The land is filled with His glory", and [Yirmiyahu 23:24] "Surely I fill the heavens and the earth." and [Tehillim 113] "Who is like Hashem ... Who sits on high and lowers Himself to view the heavens

Closeness to Hashem

and in the earth", and, "Hashem is elevated yet lowers Himself, and is high from distance of knowledge" [the former two pesukim that the Mesillat Yesharim brings are to prove the first principle that His presence exists in every place, and the latter two pesukim come to prove the principle that Hashem observes everything in the world.]

3.

When it is clear to a person that wherever he is, he stands before Hashem's Holy Presence, then automatically he will have awe and the fear within him, lest his deeds not be fitting before the height of His glory. That is what is said [in the mishna in massechet Avot - chapter 2: mishna 1], "Know what is above you; an eye that sees, an ear that listens and all your deeds are in the book of records", Since the supervision of Hashem is over everything, and He sees everything and hears everything, it is certain that all one's deeds will make an impression be recorded in a book - either as a credit or as a debt.

4.

This matter can only be pictured well in a person's intellect with regular meditation and serious thought because the matter is very distant from our senses. The mind can only possibly imagine it after much contemplation and in-depth thought. Even after the principles are understood, if one

Closeness to Hashem

doesn't constantly review it, the image will very easily disappear. Just as contemplation is the way to acquire awe, so too, lack of focus and deficiency in deep reflection are the main causes of it being lost, whether it be due to worry or purposely done. Any ceasing of concentration in this matter will put an end to any incessant awe.

5.
This is what The Holy One Blessed Be He told to a king [Devarim 17:19] "And it should be with him and he should read from it all the days of his life, so that he learn to fear Hashem." Here we learn that fear is only learnt from reading without break. Notice that it says, "So that he learns to fear…" and not, "So that he will fear…" because this fear is not within the sensations of nature, in fact it is quite the opposite and very far from it. The senses are physical, and this awe of Hashem is only acquired through unceasing study, and great diligence in Torah and it's ways.

6.
A person must ponder and think deeply about this matter. Hashem's presence is in every place and he literally stand before Him at every moment and at every time. Then a person will truly fear Him. This is what David Hamelech prayed for, "Hashem, teach me your ways, I will go in your truth with my heart to fear your name."

Closeness to Hashem

7.
The words of the Mesillat Yesharim in chapter 25 quoted above, are fundamental principles which have the power to bring a person to high and great spiritual levels. Fortunate is the one who is able to, without promises or commitments, learn this chapter of Mesillat Yesharim every day. It is certain that this will greatly improve his ways, especially if he will understand this chapter well. [See the Shulchan Aruch Yoreh Deah 214, where he writes about getting oneself used to a good habit. One should say before he begins that it is all without promises. He explains that apart from saying that it is without any promises, he should also detail that he is not committing himself to it, see well all the words inside the text itself. For reasons for this see the Levush and the Aruch Hashulchan there, what they write at length about this topic, in Nedarim 15. There is no place here to bring the whole discussion.]

8.
The essence of the words of the Mesillat Yesharim brought here is, in short, a) two principles; the first being that a person is always standing before his Creator, and the second, that every detail of his actions and business is supervised at every moment by the Creator of the world, whether it be a good deed or Hashem forbid the opposite. All his affairs in their every detail will receive

Closeness to Hashem

reckoning.

Chapter Seventeen

The Great Benefits for the Entire Jewish Nation Resulting from every Individual's Cautiousness in Areas of Sanctity and Modesty (Tzniut)

Part 1

1.
In areas of sanctity and modesty, halachic detail is brought at length in halachic and ethical works, as well as the great obligation to take care for every pitfall in transgressions in these areas. Great is the merit and the reward of one who is cautious in this, and Hashem forbid for the converse. There is no place here to discuss this further here. Here just one detail is discussed, on the topic of the benefit that there is for the entire Jewish nation from the care taken by every individual in these areas.

Closeness to Hashem

2.
It is written in Tehillim about the splitting of the sea using the expression, 'The Sea saw and fled'. Chazal explain that the sea saw the coffin of Yosef and explained with a 'gezeira shava' comparing the expression of 'fleeing' which is used with Yosef when he fled from sin, to the expression of fleeing used here. They therefore explain that the merit which caused the sea to split was that of Yosef when he restrained himself from sin. We find more on the matter in the 'Tikunei HaZohar' where he explains that had he not withstood the test, the Jews would have drowned in the Red Sea. [There is what to ponder about the promise that was made to Avraham Avinu, and there are a few ways to resolve this, no place here for elaboration.]

3.
The restraint of Yosef from sin was in the topics of this very chapter. His test was very great. Yosef was a young boy, kidnapped away from home, with no one who knew him or who wanted to help him. Chazal tell us that there was a dread within him that were he to refuse, he would be put in prison for the rest of his life, like they actually did in the end. They imprisoned him for twelve years which was already a great trial, but there was more than this. Usually there would have been no hope that he ever leaves prison, and normally he should

Closeness to Hashem

have been destined to spend the rest of his life alone, and to die in prison alone, without his family. Had he actually gone ahead and sinned, naturally speaking, it would seem that no one would ever know about it apart from the two involved. He would have carried on his profitable life trusted as the chief servant of the great prince, able to advance in every area of success in life. However, due to his fear of Hashem he held himself back from sinning. This strength split the sea and saved the entire Jewish nation.

4.

In the end he miraculously acquired royalty and as a result returned to live with his father etc. etc. It was only because he held himself back from sinning that he met the chief butler and explained his dream, who then told Pharaoh about him, who brought him to incredible success. From a simple, superficial, present viewing eye, looking at Yosef in prison, it would seem that nothing would ever become of him.

5.

We see that in the merit of an individual's cautiousness from sinning, the entire Jewish nation was saved. Here we spoke about restraint from a proper transgression, but we find that there is a unique power as a result of any good conduct in areas of sanctity, pouring blessings upon every Jew as will be explained soon in part 2 about

Closeness to Hashem

Kimchit.

6.

Chazal reveal to us that in the merit of Yosef everyone was saved, as they explain from the pesukim. According to this the many individual Jews who, throughout the generations were vigilant in these areas, must have brought about salvation and deliverance for many Jews.

7.

Kimchit's sons all merited to become high priests. It was obvious to whoever saw her sons, that the behavior of this woman had brought merit to the Jews. Chazal connect the fact that her sons were so elevated, to become high priests, to her behaviour in areas of modesty and sanctity. Accordingly, we learn that the carefulness of Jewish women throughout the generations in areas of modesty has in fact brought much deliverance and salvation for many Jews.

Closeness to Hashem

Part 2

1.
We find more in Chazal about the carefulness of Kimchit in areas of modesty, and how this brought blessing to the Jewish nation. The gemora in Yuma 47a writes, "Kimchit had seven sons who all served as high priests. The wise men asked her, 'How did you merit this?', she replied, 'Never did the walls of my house ever see the hairs of my head.' The wise men replied and said, 'Many others also did this and didn't achieve what you have!?' There is however a proof that Chazal did accept her words.

2.
In the Talmud Yerushalmi we find various places in Yuma 5a, and in Megillah 1a and in Horayot 3b which don't explain like the Talmud Bavli, and it says that the Chachamim did accept her words that she merited to this through her caution. A pasuk is brought to support this - see there.

3.
It could even be that the Talmud Bavli does not differ with the Talmud Yerushalmi. Whatever the case the wise men always agreed that this merit of

Closeness to Hashem

Kimchit was the ruling factor in regards to her special merit. The Bavli simply means to say that this merit alone cannot suffice; it must be that she had some other private merit, or have inherited some merit from her ancestors. Still her merit was certainly the main causative one. Perhaps this explanation will do well to minimize the differences of opinion especially as the argument here is about something factual. [See what the Rashash notes on the sugya, how he brings from other cases where it mentions that many others did the same thing but didn't achieve the same result. In these areas it is certain that the merit greatly helped, even though it was not sufficient and could not have been the sole reason]. Even were we to say that it is a direct argument, still the gemorah quotes all her words, and in a bartering way, pushing her words aside with only the proof that others had done the same and yet still not merited the same, meaning that there is logic in what Kimchit said. In any case the Yerushalmi definitely accepts her logic and the wise men accepted her words.

4.
What is so great about the fact that the walls of her house did not see Kimchit's hair? If it means to say that she never exposed her hair in front of males, this is a clear halacha which all women surely kept. The gemarah does not say that this

Closeness to Hashem

was reason either. What Kimchit was saying was that she never uncovered her hair, even when she was completely alone. This is something that is basically impossible to do. However, Kimchit managed this difficult thing, investing monumental effort for the sake of modesty, thereby meriting to so much. This is not a new understanding of the gemarah. It is essentially written in the gemora, in the words, "**Never** did the walls of my house see the hairs of my head."

5.

The magnitude of the merit of one's son becoming a high priest, never mind having seven sons becoming high priests, is indescribable. The high priest holds the most unique and responsible position in the entire Jewish nation. He is the one who brings atonement to the nation and he is the only one permitted and indeed commanded to enter the holiest place in the world, on the holiest day of the year. There he would perform the service on behalf of the Jewish nation. In truth he would do service in the Holy Temple on behalf of the entire nation every day of the year, according to Torat Hakabbalah. Kimchit therefore in fact succeeded in bringing great merit to every single Jew, as part of the entire nation.

6.

Even though the gemarah mentions only one detail of her modesty, we learn from this the

Closeness to Hashem

general greatness in every halacha and area of modesty and sanctity. This applies equally to men and women. [The Yerushalmi brings another good habit of Kimchit, thus implying that her merit was in the general area of modesty.]

7.

With we see Kimchit clearly how her ways brought merit to the whole Jewish nation, through her sons becoming high priests. We will explain soon just what the exact connection is between Kimchit's actions and her resulting merits. Still we can already learn from here how the many vigilances in areas of modesty that Jewish women throughout the generations took upon themselves, brought great salvations for many Jews.

Closeness to Hashem

Part 3

1.
We have seen in parts 1 and 2 the power of being careful in areas of sanctity and modesty to bring down outpourings of deliverance and salvation for the entire Jewish nation. One must question why this strength is especially connected to areas of sanctity and modesty. In truth this is already explained at length in chapter 4, that really every mitzvah and distancing from sin that a Jew performs, results in salvations for the entire Jewish nation. This is because the good influences descending from the higher worlds are increased. We saw earlier in parts 1 and 2 just how far reaching this is, and how in these areas, every action of even an individual is much more powerful.

2.
We can explain this according to hidden understandings in many ways. It is hard to speak at length about things connected to the secrets of the Torah, but we will explain here, Hashem willing, one understanding of this, according to a fundamental and great principle brought in

Closeness to Hashem

Kabbalistic works in various places. What is brought here is mainly from 'Adir Bamorom' of the Ramchal in his essay on 'Yichud Hagan', the language there is relatively easy to understand [it is interesting to know that there is a letter from the Gaon ... a disciple of R' Chaim Volozhin (and he himself was one of the greatest men in the world and his words are brought in the Mishna Berura) testifying in the name of R' Chaim Volozhin in the name of the Vilna Gaon the incredible greatness of the Ramchal in areas of Kabbalah. Furthermore, in a letter, it was said to R' Chaim about the book 'Adir Bamarom' of the Ramchal, that it is entirely revelations from the upper worlds, especially the essay on 'Yichud Hagan' which is boundlessly awesome. R' Chaim replied saying that this is certainly true. The rest of this topic is discussed later in the aforementioned work.]

3.
That is what we have discussed earlier about the way Hashem programmed the worlds, how through mitzvot and good deeds that the Jewish nation perform in this world, many higher worlds receive their rectification. As a result of this, spiritual and physical bounty descends to the Jewish nation in this world. The problem is that protection is required to ensure that this bounty reaches only goodness and that impure higher

Closeness to Hashem

powers not take it or nurture from it. It is clear from the Ramchal that this is a very big problem, and that due to this only part of the bounty descends to this world. A very large part remains in the higher worlds so that it remains preserved. It is preserved for the Jewish nation in the world to come as there is no other way to preserve it - see the Ramchal. He brings further that if one has a way to preserve the bounty it is a tremendous merit that through it, the great bounty can come to the Jewish nation in this world. [This does not in any way minimize the bounty of the next world, rather this additional bounty which descends, greatly helps to increase the merits - note his words well and you will see how this comes out from them.]

4.
Now it is proper for us to inquire as to whether we have some idea how to boost this safeguard, resulting in abundant bounty descending to the Jewish nation. One who looks carefully in the Torat HaKabbalah will see that there is a clear answer for this. This safeguard is formed through diligence to guard the laws of sanctity and modesty, whether through the carefulness of males in areas relevant to them, or the carefulness of females in areas relevant to them. Indeed any type of caution in these areas has a special and incredibly immense power to strenghten this

Closeness to Hashem

safeguard. The reason why it is especially the mitzvah of modesty which increases this safeguard is difficult to explain here in detail since it is a long and complicated topic. We will however explain a little very briefly here. I hope that whoever is familiar with Kabbalistic ideas will understand these things. The main safeguard is dependent on the keeping of limited countings of the upper countings which have connection with the power called 'The Original Snake' and anything similar to it. This in particular is dependant on the topic of modesty.

5.

With this we can understand how appropriate these warnings are to benefit the general welfare of the Jewish people. There is much Torah studied and many mitzvot performed throughout the Jewish nation, whether between man and Hashem or between man and his fellow. There are also plentiful prayers and all wonderful types of service of Hashem, all producing great bounty which has the power to activate salvations for the entire Jewish nation in literally every area. But part of all this bounty is prevented from descending to pour goodness over the Jewish people in this world due to the aforementioned powers of evil. This bounty is therefore saved for the future. Through vigilance in areas of sanctity and modesty a safeguard is produced thereby

Closeness to Hashem

enabling the bounty which was already produced and preserved, from the Jewish nations' serving of Hashem, to then descend to this world. It's really something quite easy as this bounty does not need to be produced for the Jewish nation; it is already there, waiting to be given the opportunity to join the Jewish people.

6.

This was what could bring about the splitting of the sea and the success of the service of the high priests, since these are matters of salvation for all the Jews. It was necessary to use the merits of the entire Jewish nation as well as the aforementioned safeguards in areas of modesty. The power of outstanding individuals, the strength coming from the merits of the entire Jewish nation can also affect good and blessing in spirituality and physicality in this world for the Jewish nation.

Closeness to Hashem

Part 4

1.
From all that has been said it is clear that a person must stir himself to take great care in the areas of sanctity and modesty. This can be either because of the greatness of the mitzvah, or Hashem forbid to the opposite, or because of the benefits for himself. [In truth every mitzvah or Hashem forbid it's opposite, contains benefit for the entire Jewish nation as detailed in chapter 4].

2.
A person could also be moved to do this when he thinks of the unique and mighty power that lies in matters of sanctity and modesty to bring salvation for the Jewish people. This must greatly arouse a person, whether because he wants to bring pleasure to his Creator, since it certainly brings huge pleasure to Hashem when a person spiritually and physically assists the whole of the Jewish nation, or it could arouse one's feelings of mercy for the Jewish people, for an overall deliverance or for individual salvations, which so many are waiting for. It goes without saying that when a person merits to benefit the general

Closeness to Hashem

community, his heaven-sent reward is tremendous and eternal.

3.

Rashi speaks in masechet Avodah Zarah about general care against transgressions. He says that there are two types of vigilance. The first is at the time when the opportunity presents itself, to restrain oneself not to Hashem forbid slip up. The second is to be vigilant in the first place to prevent oneself as much as possible from coming into a testing situation. This is true in every area, but even more so when it comes to matters of sanctity and modesty. It is not sufficient that a person arrange that he remain completely holy and pure, rather he must arrange his deeds and business in a way that he will not come to a situation which will test him for a deficiency or imperfection in his holiness and purity. A person must therefore sort out his matters that he not enters places or situations which cause him to stumble. It is hard to bring details here on this topic, but in a general way it is possible to say that the best advice for most people is to try as much as possible to be in the Bet Knesset and Bet Medrash. These are places which protect a person from harm, and there a person can busy himself with the holy Torah, which is the greatest possible protection from harmful things.

Closeness to Hashem

4.
In particular, when a person is in doubt not just as to how to spend a certain amount of time, but also when settling one's future, one must definitely take care that sanctity and modesty be a large factor in the decision. For example, when it comes to a career, one should arrange as best he can to spend as much time as possible in the Bet Knesset and Bet Medrash, busying himself with Torah.

5.
There are places where if a person wishes to take care in areas of sanctity and modesty in their every halachic detail, people will mock him. A person need not be embarrassed before his mockers, as we find in the Shulchan Aruch at the beginning of Ohr Hachaim, "A person should know that the truth is with him, that we heed only the wisdom of our holy Torah, and in the world to come all those who mocked him will realize his righteousness that he kept Torah, and will thank him for his vigilance in it, which shielded and protected them so much." His caution will greatly benefit the whole Jewish nation.

6.
On the rare occasions when people in his town or society poke fun at the way he performs the halachot, it would be good for him to move neighborhood or change friends so that he not

Closeness to Hashem

come to a difficult situation. It is however difficult, for various reasons, to make general rule for this, since there are situations where for other reasons the move is not good for him. The necessary requirement is that the mocking not cause him to humble or lower his level of sanctity and modesty. It is hard to bring a final judgment here without knowing the details of every individual situation.

Closeness to Hashem

Chapter Eighteen

The Prohibition of Haughtiness

1.
In the Nefesh Hachaim in the additional chapters between sha'ar 3 and sha'ar 4, he writes [adapted], "You the reader, here is your guidance, with Hashem's help, in the ways of truth, to show you the way that you should safely go. You will then be able to slowly rise through the aforementioned levels, according to the purity of your soul and according to your aspirations, more than what is laid out before you here, and also according to one's habit. You will see with your very own eyes that whatever you make a habit of, from all these levels, will add purity onto your previous purity, though engaging oneself in Torah and performing mitzvot, and in the fear and love of Hashem."

2.
We see therefore that one must guard and take great care that one's self-opinion not overtake nor

Closeness to Hashem

lift him up from serving his Creator with purity of thought. A person should not feel haughty from this. One must search and investigate this very much. It is written clearly, "Any haughtiness of heart is an abomination before Hashem" (Mishlei 17). This is even if the haughtiness is not apparent to others, only within his own heart, it is still a disgrace before Hashem, and as is well-known, is the source and the cause for all bad character traits.

3.

It is written in the gemarah that one who is proud is as if he built a forbidden private alter, and the presence of Hashem wails over it. It also says in Pesachim 66b, "Whoever is proud, if he was a wise person, his wisdom is removed from him."

4.

Whoever has fear of Hashem within him will tear the hair of his head and bring tears to his eyes when he takes to heart from who Chazal teach this principle; Hillel the Elder, who is described in the words of Chazal for his unbelievable humility. Despite this, it occurred once that it seemed he raised himself high and was punished for this immediately; the halacha was hidden from him [Pesachim 66]. What can we say, and what can we speak about. We need to investigate and inspect for this at every moment. (End of adapted quote from the Nefesh Hachaim)

Closeness to Hashem

5.
See at length the great severity of the prohibition of haughtiness in the gemarah and in ethical works. Although we can not elaborate here, we can only bring a little to awaken ourselves that a person, strengthen himself in the service of Hashem, and not come to haughtiness.

Closeness to Hashem

Chapter Nineteen

The Prohibition of Anger

1.
The gemarah and the Zohar deal very severely with the prohibition of becoming angry - see Nedarim 22 and Pesachim 66, and that which is brought in sha'arei Kedusha, part 2: sha'ar 4, in the name of the Zohar - there is no place here to elaborate further.

2.
It is written in the book 'Sha'ar Ruach Hakodesh' of Harav Chaim Vital in the name of the Arizal [p10b] [adapted] that the character trait of anger apart from entirely blinding one's comprehension, as we find on the posuk, "And Moshe was angry with Elozor and Itamar...", Chazal say that whoever becomes angry, if he is a prophet, his prophesy is removed from him, if he is wise, his wisdom is removed from him [Pesachim 66b].

Closeness to Hashem

3.
It is even worse than this, as we will explain. The Arizal was very particular in the area of anger, more than all other transgressions, even when he would be angry for the sake of a mitzvah, like in the case with Moshe brought earlier. He would reason that all other aveirot do not entirely disable, rather each aveirah blemishes one limb. Anger, however, wounds the entire soul and alters it completely. The point here is that when a person becomes irritated the holy soul completely withdraws from him, and in its place comes a soul from the 'exterior' (lower) side - this is a hidden matter - the pasuk speaks about this, "He tears his soul with his anger" [Iyov 18]. At the time of anger and fury, it literally tears out his holy soul and leaves it torn, killing it. And as the Zohar brings in parshat Tetzaveh p182b. how much the Zohar stresses the topic of anger, so much so that one who is together with an angry person is as if he is right next to an idol - see the text inside

4.
Even if a person makes rectifications to his soul and does a fantastic repentance for all his sins, and does numerous and great mitzvot, it is all completely lost to him. The holy soul which did all those good deeds has been exchanged for an impure one and left him, leaving the impure maidservant in its place to inherit its mistress. It

Closeness to Hashem

requires that he return again and correct all that the original corrections that he did. This happens every time that he is angry because an angry person cannot receive rectification at all; he is like a dog that repeatedly eats his own vomit.

5.

He also damages himself in another way. This is that it could be that he did some great mitzvah which brought down the soul of a righteous person to come to help him. Now due to the anger, this also departs from him. This is another part of the meaning of the soul being torn.

6.

As long as a person has the trait of anger, he can never reach any spiritual heights, even though he may be righteous in every other area, since he builds and then when he become angry immediately destroys all that he has just built. Other transgressions do not tear out and uproot the soul, although they remain stuck to it. They are however blemishes in the aspect of that aveirah alone. When he corrects that blemish it is entirely fixed. But anger requires numerous rectifications and much preparation to return his soul that was ripped away from him. Perhaps, as we find in the Zohar in parshat Tezaveh, according to the type and essence of the anger, sometimes it cannot be fixed at all. Even more than this, my teacher would rebuke me greatly even for the times that I would

Closeness to Hashem

get angry with my brother whilst teaching him.

7.

When it is written that the aveirah of anger is the most severe in the Torah because of the departure of the soul, it refers to the severity from one specific aspect. Of course, from other aspects there are transgressions more severe than anger. Obviously if a person is forced to choose between desecrating Shabbat or to become angry, he must choose the option of anger and not desecrate the Shabbat. Not only with Shabbat, which is more severe, but with all other transgressions too, there is no way that one can slip up in a particular prohibition in order to hold himself back from becoming angry, even though there is a unique gravity with anger. There are of course many other sides to this and therefore there is no leeway to fall into any prohibition in order to save oneself from anger.

8.

There is another very severe thing about anger. Apart from anger itself being very serious, the fact is that an angry person is very likely to harm others with his words. One must take great care with this because there is a Torah prohibition of paining someone with words - see what is written about this earlier in chapter 11.

Chapter Twenty

The Advantages of Studying Torah and Serving Hashem with Joy and Excitement

1.
The Gaon R' Chaim Volozhin writes in a letter [printed at the end of the augmented version of the Nefesh Hachaim p421] about how Torah study is something which needs constant encouragement. "I have never held back from encouraging you and from hurrying a conscientious person to learn Torah with alacrity and great enthusiasm, because what one learns lazily taking a whole day, he can learn in just a few hours were he to learn with zeal…
2.
…The thoughts of your heart should always be on words of Torah. Even whilst eating and sleeping, one's thoughts should be on words of Torah.

Closeness to Hashem

One's studies should also be in Torah, so that the words of Torah are constantly in one's mouth" - see the text of the Nefesh Hachaim for further details.

3.
Harav Chaim Vital writes in his book 'Sha'ar Ruach Hakodesh'[p.10b] in the name of the Arizal, "Whenever a person performs a mitzvah, or is engaged in Torah or in prayer, he should be happier and merrier than one who has earned or found many thousands of golden dinars." See all his words inside. He means to say here that this is the correct way to serve Hashem, since the happiness shows how important the service of Hashem is to him. [However, he does not mean to say that if a person has no way to be happy, he should still not slacken in his service of Hashem. He should always do as much as he can manage.]

4.
Torah should be studied with great joy, as should the performance of all mitzvot be. R' Chaim Vital adds that by learning with enthusiasm and happiness, it usually helps the success of the study, see what is written in the letter mentioned in point 1 above.

5.
Know that excitement and happiness in Torah study, and in other areas of serving Hashem, greatly sanctify and purify a person's soul, for

Closeness to Hashem

many reasons. One reason is that a person has many layers in his soul and often when a person serves his Creator, it grasps and strengthens only part of these layers, and the other layers participate less. But when he learns Torah or serves Hashem in any matter, with excitement and zeal, more layers of the soul are used in this learning and mitzvah performance. The happiness also affects deeper layers of his soul and as a result he is greatly purified.

Closeness to Hashem

Chapter 21

References in Other Works Relevant to the Topics Discussed in this Book

All the topics in "Words of encouragement for the study of gemarah" are relevant to this work.

There are various points relevant to this work in my commentary on the Torah, mainly in parshat Vayeitzei, parshat Metzorah, parshat Acharei-mot, pashat Emor, parshat Behar, parshat Vayelech, parshat Vezot-haberacha and various other places.

In my work on Neviim and Kesubim there are relevant points in Yirmiyahu (chapter 32) and in Yoel (chapter 2) and a few other places too.

There are very many connecting points in my commentary on Agadot.

Closeness to Hashem

The entire work on the collection of matters in areas of ethics, from the Vilna Gaon is very relevant to this work.

Similarly the essays, "Mordechai Ha'alyah" and, "Ma'alot Hakedusha" are connected to this work.

www.ingramcontent.com/pod-product-compliance
Lightning Source LLC
Chambersburg PA
CBHW070145080526
44586CB00015B/1853